Beyond Comfort

Beyond Comfort

Mastering a Growth Mindset with Excellence Through Urgency

Ted Rath

©2024 All Rights Reserved. No portion of this book may be reproduced, stored in a retrieval system, or transmitted in any form or by any means—electronic, mechanical, photocopy, recording, scanning, or other—except for brief quotations in critical reviews or articles without the prior permission of the author.

Published by Game Changer Publishing

Paperback ISBN: 978-1-964811-73-4
Hardcover ISBN: 978-1-964811-74-1
Digital ISBN: 978-1-964811-75-8

www.GameChangerPublishing.com

DEDICATION

To Robin, Brooklyn, Brady, and Emmy.
You allow me to chase my dreams while inspiring me
to aim even higher. THANK YOU!
We are just getting started!!

Read This First

Just to say thanks for buying and reading my book, scan the code below for additional resources and a free offering.

Scan the QR Code Here:

Beyond Comfort

*Mastering a Growth Mindset
with Excellence Through Urgency*

Ted Rath

www.GameChangerPublishing.com

Foreword

Ted Rath is a warrior who prepares other warriors for battle.

He is uniquely qualified to write *Beyond Comfort* as a man who has stepped on countless football battlefields, first as a walk-on at the University of Toledo and for the past two decades as a leader in the sports performance industry.

Through his hard work and dedication to principles he has gathered and cultivated over time, Ted has risen through the ranks and received numerous accolades. That includes twice being named the NFL Strength and Conditioning Coach of the Year, as the inaugural president of the Professional Football Performance Coaches Association, and as a vice president for the Eagles, among many others. His successes are a direct result of applying what he has learned in the trenches for the better part of twenty years.

I met Ted through our work together for the Los Angeles Rams and the Philadelphia Eagles, where we were part of a larger and successful effort to guide both teams to Super Bowl appearances. We quickly became friends through our mutual respect and a shared vision of the strategies and principles of what it takes to succeed on the field and in life.

Two of the most important lessons you'll read more about are on the following pages. They're worth mentioning here because of how foundational they are as part of Ted's peak performance philosophy.

The first is that iron sharpens iron and focuses on the relationships essential to growth that challenge you through adversity. Ted and I both understand that adversity is uncomfortable but is necessary for growth in your life.

The second of these is working to a championship standard. Ted is a huge proponent of creating uncompromising ways of doing things and consistently working through processes that directly impact results defined by that standard. Ted expands on why this mindset is so critical for your success and directly aligns with my philosophy, which I also explained in detail in my book, *The Standard*.

We push others to seek out the uncomfortable parts of their lives, but we also push each other to find the uncomfortable parts of our lives, too. We know that part of our close friendship is built on being honest with each other so that we can better rise to any occasion as teachers, mentors, and motivators.

Ted also understands that there is no margin for error when you're in the trenches every week. As you'll learn, preparing men for battle in front of millions of rabid fans requires complete transparency. There is no place to hide, and while you're measured by the results on the scoreboard, winning games starts long before you ever step on the field. The part you don't see is often more important than the part you do see.

Only the best can work in this kind of arena. Even fewer can do it for as long and as well as Ted has done.

When you read *Beyond Comfort*, understand that Ted's "total commitment" is more than just a phrase he utters to fire up players. It is a way of life from one of the most impressive warriors I know.

– Ben Newman
USA Today TOP 5 Mindset & Performance Coach
2x Wall Street Journal Bestseller

Table of Contents

Introduction 1

Chapter 1 – The Standard is the Standard..................................5

Chapter 2 – Finding Congruence 29

Chapter 3 – Default Urgent..41

Chapter 4 – Telescope to Microscope 59

Chapter 5 – The Humility Habit 79

Chapter 6 – Getting Out of Your Comfort Zone......................93

Chapter 7 – The Habit of Discipline: Daily Deposits..........111

Chapter 8 – Leadership Lessons Learned 123

Conclusion..141

Introduction

My name is Ted Rath. I've worked in leadership roles in the sports performance industry for the past 18 years. The majority of my career has been spent in the National Football League; I've worked in 4 organizations and risen to the vice president level for the Philadelphia Eagles. I'm also a two-time recipient of the NFL Strength and Conditioning Coach of the Year Award. I've helped take two franchises to the Super Bowl, been on the hiring committee for an NFL head coaching search, and voted the inaugural president of the Professional Football Performance Coaches Association.

Over nearly two decades, I've learned valuable lessons from some of the top leaders in professional sports. This book gathers that knowledge for readers with the goal of helping them become the best versions of themselves.

How did I get to where I am today? Born in a small town and with a rural upbringing, my childhood was one of hard work, grit, and determination. I watched my father wake up at 2:30 in the morning to make the one-hour drive to Detroit, Michigan, to get to work on time. I also watched him come home and still be willing to coach our Little League teams and play catch with me out in the backyard.

My mother embodies what women are capable of. She once competed in the demolition derby at our county fair simply because people said a woman couldn't do it. I learned grit and determination from an early age by watching my parents work their butts off and tackle challenging opportunities with focused attitudes.

Across the field that bordered our property was my grandparents' farm. At an early age, I learned the value of hard work. Baling hay in the summer heat and humidity and doing other odd projects around the farm taught me that sweat is a commodity and that being willing to put forth effort can determine future success.

As I transitioned through high school and gained a love and appreciation for sports and training, I started to develop as an athlete. I was fortunate to play collegiate football at the University of Toledo. Division I football continued to teach me the value of dedication and daily effort. Numerous teammates realized their goal of playing in the NFL, and they all shared similar traits, primarily a strong work ethic. After my playing career, I was blessed to be able to coach and work at the University of Toledo for two years. After that, I got my start in the NFL, and while rising through the ranks, I've learned many valuable lessons from some of the best leaders in the history of the game.

I'm writing this book to help everyone understand that consistency is one of the best measurements of performance. When you apply consistent habits over time through healthy decisions and daily deposits, you become a better version of yourself. This is something that everyone should be passionate about. Can you imagine going through life with the opportunity to create better outcomes in every aspect of your existence? What would you be willing to change or exchange for an improved life? What negative habits would you be willing to edit out? What positive habits would you be willing to add if you knew that they would guarantee you a better chance of becoming the person you dream of becoming?

Well, that's what this book is for. This book will offer you simple but clear processes that you can add to your daily habits to help you accomplish your goals. We all have this opportunity in front of us. Through a series of stories and questions, this book will take you on a journey, helping you to reflect on yourself and identify the positive habits you need to lean into and the negative ones you need to edit out. It also offers simple and practical tools that anyone can apply and incorporate immediately, inspiring you to take the next steps toward becoming a better and more productive person. If you want to become a better version of yourself, this book is for you.

After reading this book and working through the exercises, I hope that you start to see stress and adversity as things that can inspire and create better outcomes for us. As you learn to lean into the stress, you will develop better patterns and pathways that will allow you to become a version of yourself that you can be proud of. Invest in yourself today. This book will help you get there.

CHAPTER 1

The Standard is the Standard

When we say, "The standard is the standard," what do we mean by this? The standard is the actions that you demonstrate through your daily habits. We all have personal standards. We all have corporate standards and cultural standards wherever we work and wherever we live. In our family, our home, our churches—in any environment in which we exist—we have standards.

Those standards are expressed in our daily actions. Your standards should be connected to your core values. If you don't have clearly defined core values, I challenge you to sit down with intentional thought and purpose and come up with a list of them that you can revisit when making key decisions throughout your life. Is your goal to perform at a higher level? If so, do your personal standards align with elite performance? I challenge you to look at your daily habits and ask yourself honestly and authentically if they align with elite-level performance. Do a self-assessment.

Ask yourself these key questions:

- Do you consistently wake up early?

- Do you hit the snooze button and sleep in?
- Are you in good physical shape?
- Do you exercise daily?
- Are you within a healthy weight range?
- Do you make sound nutritional decisions the majority of the time?
- Are you in good mental shape? (Our mental health can be more important than the physical health that we attack every single day.)
- Do you read daily?
- Do you listen to podcasts?
- Do you challenge yourself by participating in stimulating conversations that lead to growth?
- Do you surround yourself with others who share a growth mindset and truly care about making you into a better version of yourself?
- Do you practice breathwork?
- Do you have positive or negative self-talk?
- Do you practice meditation?

If you incorporate these practices into your daily habits, they will have a large impact on your future outcomes.

What about accountability?

- Do you hold yourself and others accountable in a productive way? The most important aspect of this is your self-accountability. Do you take ownership of your situation? Wherever you are, do you use humble accountability?

- Do you seek feedback from others? More importantly, do you listen to that feedback? And then, *most* importantly, do you apply that feedback and actually put it into action?

Everyone has a friend who says, "Hey, how can I do this better?" However, after receiving feedback, they don't change their actions or behaviors. Don't be that person. Show with actions. We see better than we hear. So, you can say all the right things, but if your actions are not in alignment with elite-level performance, your standards are lacking.

- How do you expect to become a better version of yourself? Make sure to demonstrate, not just say, what your standards are through your actions and behavior.

After-action reviews are one of the most important ways that we can look at self-accountability and total accountability, especially in a team or leadership environment. Who does this better than anyone? The military is one of the best organizations to study when aiming to apply more efficient after-action reviews into your daily life.

The Navy SEALS

The Navy SEALs heavily rely on after-action reviews. I've been fortunate to visit the Navy SEALs training compound at Coronado on the West Coast, where they select their recruits with BUDS. There, I spoke with some of the world's most elite operators and asked them, "What do you do better than anyone?"

Their answers typically revolved around after-action reviews. And what are they? After-action reviews are a form of accountability. The important thing to remember is that it's not just for accountability within the team. The ultimate goal is to get to the point where you are self-accountable before you hold everyone else accountable. This is something that SEALs do better than anyone else. Before they get to the point where someone can bring up a mistake, shortcoming, or failure in a mission or a training session, the person who caused that mistake will have already humbly stepped forward and said, "Hey, I messed this up, but more importantly, here are the actions that I will take to fix it, and you'll see them the next time."

Now, how do they do this? They build trust, vulnerability, and accountability throughout their very challenging training. They do hard things together. This is an important lesson for anyone trying to raise their standard. Do you participate in things that constantly challenge you? Do you dive into opportunities when they might be slightly uncomfortable, but you know it's the best thing to do because it's the right thing?

Easy does not always mean best. Actually, it often leads to the worst-case scenario. Do easy less; do hard better and more often. That will lead to higher accountability and higher standards in your daily life. The SEALs are elite; anyone who has spent time watching them train will agree. The great separator for them might be their self-accountability. When you ask SEAL team leaders what they can do better, they always give you the same answer: "We can always improve on our after-action reviews because we can always improve on accountability, both with each other and ourselves."

Avoid the Snooze

What are some other ways that you can build greater standards in your environment? You have to build your environment to be in alignment with what you want to accomplish. Is your environment built in such a way that it's haphazardly thrown together? You attempt to wake up early, but you make it easy to hit the snooze button by keeping the alarm clock next to your bed or your phone within reaching distance. If you have that habit, I challenge you to move your alarm clock. Set your phone up on the other side of the room and force yourself to get out of bed. Once again, do easy less; do hard better and more often.

This is just one simple example of how we can design our environment to improve our daily habits. If you're trying to get better at consuming podcasts to sharpen your skills, well, what are you listening to on your way to and from work if you have a commute? Stop listening to music; switch it over to a podcast. Do you work out every day? Instead of watching TV, maybe during a cardio session, throw on a podcast or throw on your headphones and try to engage in something that's going to make you into a better version of yourself.

Sean McVay—Master of Setting a Standard

One of the greatest examples of setting a standard is Sean McVay. Sean is the head coach of the Los Angeles Rams, and I was fortunate to come in with him in 2017. At the time, Sean and I were the youngest in our positions in the NFL. At 30, he was the youngest head coach in the history of the league. We were both hired to undertake this incredible responsibility of leading an NFL organization. The year prior, 2016, the Rams record was 4 and 12. The expectations from outsiders were low, but the standards that we began to incorporate within the organization would lead to a dominant run of winning that would take the NFL by storm.

Sean and I share a similar approach to reading: we try to consume as much knowledge as possible. We just so happened to be reading the book *Extreme Ownership* by Jocko Willink and Leif Babin at the same time as we began our roles in Los Angeles. We applied several of the book's lessons as we intentionally worked to build a strong culture with the team. Sean utilized the principle of decentralized command by empowering his staff. We also employed the "prioritize and execute" approach in our daily practice standards. We learned through the process of growing together; each day, we would share knowledge that we had picked up. This typically occurred during our morning workouts. As we took time to improve ourselves physically, naturally, we included the habit of sharpening our minds. We challenged each other in a positive and productive manner—both physically and mentally.

Details matter, and these daily briefs were opportunities to discuss the ones that would eventually lead to championships. We started to build our standards within the environment. We started to say, "What graphics do we need to demonstrate that our standards are going to be unique within the NFL? How do we do this around the facility?" What you see is what you get, so we were very intentional with what we put up on the walls, the wording, the phrases, and how we spoke to the team. Phrases like "The standard is the standard" and "It's all about the process" came to light because we demonstrated them in our day-to-day actions. Our daily habits aligned with what we were saying, and as we watched this trickle-down effect, eventually, it led to the players and throughout the entire organization.

As we built the culture and environment intentionally, we came up with different ways to hold players accountable. There's a fine system in place in the NFL, outlined in the Collective Bargaining Agreement. We kept the rules very simple, making them clear and concise. For example, players would be fined if they were late for a meeting, training session, practice session, or anything else that was deemed mandatory. We also instituted a fine if they were outside of their weight range. One of the first prominent moments in the development of the culture came at a moment that could have been handled in two very different ways.

Seconds Matter

In 2017, we had a player named Michael Brockers. Brock, as he was known throughout the team, was a leader with a strong voice in the locker room. He was a very influential member of the team and a great person. At an early point during training camp, our first year in 2017, we were at the University of California Irvine, where we spent several weeks during training camp each year. During one of our first days there, we held a mandatory training session in the UC Irvine weight room. The weight room has automatic glass sliding doors at the main entrance where players would enter after coming from the locker room downstairs. Brock came into the weight room one day ten seconds late. Literally ten seconds late. I can vividly picture him as he approached the glass doors. I looked at our clocks, thinking, *Come on, Brock. Don't put me in this situation.* Well, he put me in that situation.

As you think about the impact that ten seconds can have, keep your standards in mind. I could have stopped and said, "It's ten seconds, so here we are." It was one of the first sessions of training camp, so this was one of the first times that we could actually issue fines. Many don't know this, but in the offseason, you cannot issue fines until you have a mandatory minicamp. So, typically, when you report to training camp, it's the first time that you will actually issue fines.

As Brock walked in late and we were already starting, I had a choice to make. Would I uphold the standard at that moment, or would I let it slide? I said to myself, "This is going to be uncomfortable in the short term, but it's going to lead to a better outcome down the line for our team and the culture of this organization." After looking at the clock again to be sure, I said, "Brock, you're late."

"Oh, man, it's only a few seconds," he said and began to complain. At that moment, I made a split-second decision. Putting the whistle to my mouth, I blew it. This brought the entire team up. I said, "Hey, guys, remember what we talked about how the standard is the standard? We've been preaching this since the off-season began, and we've been preaching that we are going to all be accountable. You guys agreed to this. You said we need accountability and need the standards to rise. Well, this is going to be a fine for Brock. He was ten seconds late."

Once again, Brock said, "It's a couple of seconds. Does it really matter?"

The switch hit, and I said, "Does it matter if we go into the fourth quarter of a game that potentially hinges on a playoff appearance and Russell Wilson is scrambling in the backfield? We're trying to get him down to end the game because it's a fourth down, and if we get it, it's a walk-off win for us. Do we just go tap him and two-hand touch him, and the ref blows the whistle, or do we have to finish the play? We have to put him on the ground, and we have to make sure that we have finished the play so that the end of the game is certain."

As I spoke, the team began to see my passion rise and understand that standards are exactly that: they are standards. They cannot be compromised. If you compromise on one, others will follow. But when we do not compromise, we continue to build, we continue to stack, and we continue to hold each other accountable to that standard.

In the great cultures that I've been around, people not only hold each other accountable, but they hold themselves to the standard first. When it comes to self-accountability, the beauty is that it trickles down to others because it is uncomfortable to be the person who is not holding themselves accountable.

Holding Yourself Accountable

So, what happened after this moment? There were more fines down the line, not a lot, but as we began to hold to our standards, players took self-ownership. They began to say simple things like, "The standard is the standard." When other players walked in late, they'd say, "My bad. The standard is the standard. I know that's a fine, and I won't let it happen again." As this process unfolded, I saw the belief and confidence rise in the organization and team culture. Coaches, staff members, players, and front office members began to buy in and speak the same language. The most important thing, though, was that we followed through with our daily actions. The standard became the standard through consistent action. We demonstrated with our daily actions and habits what we were all preaching.

Sean did a great job of demonstrating this in other ways as well, not only by keeping very simple rules and holding players accountable but, more importantly, with his self-accountability. There was one particular instance when he had what we'll call a light argument with another coach on the field. This was during a practice session, and if you'd seen it, you might have thought, *This isn't that important*, and just brushed it off. You know, the other coach shouldn't attack the head coach like that.

Sean's head was spinning, and I could see him considering the outcomes. He was having a moment like the one I'd had with Brockers, wondering, *Do I address this? Do I not address this? How is this going to impact the standards of our team?* Then I saw a flicker in his eye, and he said, "Hey, bring everybody up."

After I blew the whistle and everyone had gathered, Sean took ownership with a sense of urgency and authenticity that reverberated throughout the team. He said, "I have to live to a higher standard. I'm your head coach. I let you down at that moment. I won't let it happen again. I won't let my emotions run away like that and get the better of me. I will show you that I will not let this happen again." After that, his actions proved true. Do people make mistakes? Yes. Do we have to offer grace when those things happen? Absolutely. But our daily standards are the most important factors in our future outcomes.

Another time Sean showed great accountability occurred after a game, our second of the season. We began the season with an impressive blowout victory over the Indianapolis Colts. It was very lopsided. The team's confidence was soaring because of the big victory that began the season. Not many people in the city or the league thought that we could accomplish great things that first year, but when we scored over 40 points in that first game, everyone took notice. The second game was an emotional one for Sean because it was against his former team, Washington. It was a tight game—it went back and forth—but ultimately, we fell short.

I could see the emotion on Sean's face after the game, and I knew that he was in a place of deep reflection because he hadn't lived up to the expectations he'd set for himself—not the team, but himself. He took complete ownership of the things that he was expected to control. After the game, the team gathered in the middle of the locker room. As we stood there, somber and silent in the bowels of the LA Coliseum, he began to speak and demonstrated his humble leadership. He brought everyone up and said, "Listen, I won't let that happen again. I allowed my emotions to take control of that game, and that will not happen again. I made it more about my personal feelings about that team and how badly I wanted that victory than about us. That will not happen again."

And from that day forward, Sean didn't let it happen again. You could see him focus and lock in, and that self-accountability allowed everyone else to take ownership of what they could control. When you have a leader who steps up and says, "Listen, I messed this up," then you have a beautiful cascade of others being willing to humbly admit when they fail or have shortcomings and then learning from those mistakes. We only fail forward. We never miss an opportunity to learn. Make sure that your standards align with ownership and accountability.

Commit to the Work

Another experience I had regarding standards happened when I was working for the Detroit Lions. This was in 2009, and it was my first season in the NFL. I'd been fortunate to get an opportunity to work for the Lions, my hometown team. I had been in a full-time position at the University of Toledo as the assistant strength and conditioning coach, but the Lions job was a part-time gig that first year, where I was limited in hours and how much I could financially earn.

If you've ever spent time working in the sport of professional football, you quickly realize that the hours are not typical. We don't work 40-hour weeks. In fact, at times of the year, we work over a hundred hours a week, and a lot of times, that pace continues for several months straight with no days off. In my first year with Detroit, our off-season training program lasted for 14 weeks. This was under a previous CBA, so we participated in a longer off-season than what we currently see in the NFL schedule. I maxed out all of my hours that off-season, so as we entered training camp, I had to sign paperwork saying, "Hey, I'm willing to work for free, and this is what I'm gonna do." I didn't receive a paycheck for 6 months until I was promoted the following February to a full-time position.

To make ends meet and produce a little bit of income to help pay bills, I did other jobs outside of the rigorous hours of an NFL coaching schedule. I began a couple of high school strength and conditioning programs for local schools. Earning the opportunity to work in the NFL is a great privilege. I recognized this every day that I attacked my opportunity. As I look back, my standards were in alignment with what my future goals were. Just because I wasn't going to get a paycheck, it didn't mean I wouldn't show up for work and put the best version of myself forward each day. Whether you are making a million dollars or volunteering for free, the attitude and standards that we show up with are 100% based on our choice. I was going to continue to put my best foot forward, stack days, stack opportunities, and make sure that, ultimately, my standards were in alignment with what my future goals were: to become a full-time strength and conditioning coach, then a head strength and conditioning coach, and eventually, to attain some of the highest positions in our profession.

Waking up early every single day when you're working for free and committing to the work are standards that align with future success. There was a point in time when I would wake up in Toledo, Ohio, and take the hour-long commute to Allen Park, Michigan, where the Detroit Lions training facility is located. After a full day of work, I would drive to Ann Arbor to build a strength and conditioning program for student-athletes at a local high school. By the time I got back home to Toledo, hopefully, I had enough time to get a few hours of sleep, and then the next day, I would wake up and repeat the cycle. Developing consistent work habits during this time showed me the value of doing so. What are you doing today to raise your personal standards?

I've been fortunate to work with players of rare talent who have combined their gifts with elite levels of hard work. I've seen their standards lead to Hall of Fame careers. These are players like Calvin Johnson, Aaron Donald, Ndamukong Suh, Andrew Whitworth, Lane Johnson, Jason Kelce, and the list goes on and on. Each of these players continues to inspire me because I was able to witness their work habits, and I saw their personal standards earn them a legacy of greatness that will be established forever in the Pro Football Hall of Fame.

The Standard of Winning

I've always found that most people are more willing to accept coaching in the midst of a loss. Typically, when dealing with the effects of a loss, it is easier to remain humble and look inwardly at what you can and should change moving forward. When you are actively winning and achieving your goals, it becomes easier to overlook the minor errors and small mistakes. Basically, winning covers up mistakes. I've seen this at a high level in professional sports. In my experience, it's more difficult to maintain higher standards in the midst of winning streaks. I have been fortunate to be a part of the last remaining undefeated team in the NFL on multiple occasions. In 2018 with the Los Angeles Rams and in 2022 with the Philadelphia Eagles, we started both of those seasons 8–0. This made us the last team with an unblemished record in each of those years. With that came a significantly sized bullseye from the competition.

When a team is on a losing streak, everyone feels a sense of urgency to improve. What happens when you become the standard? Unfortunately, many times, it is a slow and steady decline that comes from ignoring the art of maintaining a growth mindset. When small mistakes go uncorrected, it begins a slow unraveling of the standards that allowed you to get into the winning column in the first place.

Most likely, you will not recognize this at first. As the first loss comes, sometimes, you will even offer up excuses and nonchalantly accept them. I offer a strict warning: this is the beginning of your new standard… a losing standard. The standard must not come from a result-based goal; your winning standard must be rooted in the daily process. In each of those seasons when we were the last remaining unbeaten team, our standards rose to the level of our preparation. It wasn't easy to maintain focus on the process at times, but it was the most important thing that we could do. And it was the RIGHT thing to do if we wanted to continue our winning ways.

When it comes to dealing with adversity in our daily lives, there are three groups of people. First are those who are currently in the middle of dealing with some form of adversity. They are actively working through a problem to some degree. Second, some have just come out of an adverse situation and are trying to navigate their path back to elite performance. Last, some are about to enter into another bout of adversity. These are people who have been collecting win after win. They are in the zone; they are dominating their role and seem to have everything under control. These are the undefeated teams and individuals that we see performing at an incredibly high level.

When you find yourself in this third group, the standard with which you operate becomes absolutely critical. Jim Collins, an incredible author whose books have sold more than 10 million copies worldwide, eloquently writes about maintaining productive paranoia in his book *Good to Great*. This is a perfect expression for these moments. These are the times in our lives when we must double down on the process; while we do so, our standards must be rooted in disciplined daily habits. As we learn to zoom in and out of each situation that we find ourselves in, we must attack the standards of our daily disciplines with a relentless focus. Our attitude is OUR choice; our efforts are OUR choice. Once we grasp this reality and embrace the power that it brings, we can truly live to the STANDARD!

The Rocket Rep Standard

During my college football career, I learned one of the most valuable lessons about setting and following a standard of excellence. Entering the University of Toledo as a walk-on athlete allowed me to develop one of the biggest mentor relationships of my life. Our head strength and conditioning coach, Steve Murray, demonstrated the standard in more ways than one.

First, he is one of the most respectful and humble individuals I have ever encountered. His personal standards for how he approaches life as a Christian, husband, and father are more notable than his professional accomplishments. That being said, he has achieved an impressive collection of championships and accolades during his multiple decades leading several teams at the University of Toledo.

One thing that reminds me of the simplicity of creating a standard is the "Rocket Rep." The repetition is the foundation of strength training. Every player who has reached the pinnacle of their sport and plays professionally has only achieved the necessary skill to do so through the continuous application of practice reps. In strength training, it is no different. In a given workout, the number of sets and the total amount of time spent training can differ; applying the ideal amount of repetitions is what is critically important. With so many repetitions required, it becomes easy to get lethargic and simply go through the motions. This was not the case in those early days when I learned the value of establishing a one-rep-at-a-time approach, not only to strength training but also in life.

As I type this, I'm staring at the four-page document that defines the perfect Toledo Rocket Rep. Every repetition has three distinct phases, and this document clearly and concisely defines each one: the lifting (concentric) phase, the contraction (isometric) phase, and the lowering (eccentric) phase. Neglecting any of these phases will lessen the overall effectiveness of the repetition. However, from the optimist's perspective, optimizing each phase will allow you to make significant gains in your strength and power abilities. When taking this perspective, each rep becomes an opportunity.

Many opportunities in life are missed because we lose focus on the things we can control. By breaking down our daily standards into manageable repetitions, we can gain clarity and simplicity in a step-by-step approach that will lead us to incredible growth. We used the rocket rep to our advantage; I still use this rep-by-rep approach to my personal advantage. When you choose to see the path to success as a one-rep-at-a-time process, your standards will allow you to achieve incredible results over time.

While the rep was the foundation of what we accomplished in our workouts, the standard was more evident in the effort we put into every workout. We trained with a method known as H.I.T., or high-intensity training. This is vastly different from H.I.I.T., or high-intensity interval training, which many people have become invested in. The H.I.T. training that we undertook was based on a phrase that revolves around a good kind of failure. What type of failure can be considered good? With a growth mindset, any and every single failure can and should bring us a little bit closer to our goals. So, in that sense, every failure that we encounter is a good thing. We fail FORWARD!

The failure that was applied to our strength training workouts revolved around momentary muscular failure. Here's a very simple explanation to save you from reading an additional 30 pages. Training with the H.I.T. method typically requires one set per exercise to complete and momentary muscular failure. This means literally giving an all-out effort into every rep of every single set throughout your workout. Because we were training to "failure," equipment selection was incredibly important to maintain safety. Machines rather than free weights like barbells were often used to maximize safety and efficiency. With any given set of upper-body exercises, the goal was to select a weight that would allow you to perform somewhere between six to 12 perfect repetitions. This would allow momentary muscular failure to occur around the 40-second mark. For the lower body, since the muscles are much larger, we would select a weight and timeframe that allowed momentary failure to occur around the 60- to 70-second mark.

As you read these words, think about what it means to completely deplete your energy system of its ability to move a weight and then continue to push as hard as humanly possible to get through the next inch of movement. This summarizes the type of training that we embraced. Reps were slow and controlled, and the weight felt heavier with each repetition. Then, as you approached failure, your spotter would lend a supporting hand only during the concentric phase.

Due to gravity, we are able to lower significantly more weight during the eccentric phase of each exercise. Because of this, once we had established momentary muscular failure during the concentric phase, we were still able to lower the weight in a slow and controlled manner for several more repetitions. So, the spotter would help during the raising phase so we could forcefully squeeze the targeted muscles in the contraction phase. Once the weight had been lifted, the spotter would stop helping, and it was the duty of the lifter to lower the weight in a controlled manner; this allowed further inroads into the muscular recruitment pathways as the body's system called for additional motor units to help with the intense and uncomfortable work.

As I type this, the memories flood back of highly challenging workouts, and the numerous times I found myself visiting a trash can to recycle my breakfast after embracing the failure challenge a little bit too much. But the most memorable aspect of those challenging times is the lesson I learned about embracing a standard of EFFORT! As each rep became more difficult, I found myself in a mental negotiation with terrorists. In this case, the terrorists that I was negotiating with were the sabotaging villains of laziness!

We've all had this negotiation; it doesn't always come in the form of a challenging workout. Sometimes, it surfaces because of doubt or a sudden case of imposter syndrome. This terrorist can come in times of victory or during times of weakness and defeat. In fact, we often make our greatest gains in the midst of failure and defeat. As we embrace failure, we must choose to zoom out and refocus on how we look at it. We can see this failure as an opportunity for growth. We can embrace the discomfort that will ultimately forge us into becoming a better version of our previous selves. This is a CHOICE! This is OUR choice!

The Standard of Players

Calvin Johnson is one of the most dedicated people that I've ever had the chance to work with. Calvin, or CJ, as we call him, is one of the best athletes I have ever been around. He is also one of the greatest human beings and one of the most humble people that I have ever been fortunate to call a friend. CJ would come into work every single day, and his habits were consistently aligned with those of a Hall of Fame-caliber player. One of the greatest players ever at his position, he led by example every day.

The one story about CJ that I fondly remember was when he asked about a specific daily soft-tissue exercise that I had shown him earlier in his career. I soon discovered that CJ had followed this exact protocol every single day since—and he'd done it for years. He embodies the phrase, "How you do one thing is how you do everything." This is the type of consistency that it takes to become a Hall of Fame player. He didn't just do it for one day; he stacked days, and it became his personal standard.

Aaron Donald is another person who comes to mind when I think of incredible standards demonstrated every day. AD's physical work habits are rare, but many people don't realize that his film study habits and how he prepared for opponents with an intentional discipline also made him a special player. He knew that combining urgent discipline in his physical and mental training would eventually lead to him becoming a better player, and he did this with an elite level of focus and intentionality. Aaron continued to work his butt off throughout the offseason. When the season ended, he typically took very little time off, and he was back to attacking long and intense workouts every single day. His standards were aligned with becoming one of the greatest ever at his position, much like CJ.

Another player I admire is Ndamukong Suh. His entire career has been built on his work habits and elite focus on the details of what it takes to get himself ready. It is incredible to think that a player who played well over a decade in the NFL, 13 seasons, never once missed a game due to injury. His intense focus on the details and his dedication to his personal standards led him to compete in three Super Bowls as well. He did this through repetitive work that became his consistent foundation. And what is that? Those are his standards, the things that he lives by, and the things that he puts into work every day. He's done the same thing outside of sports in some of his business ventures. His standards don't change. The setting might adjust, such as when he's on a board of directors and working through a new business acquisition or playing in an NFL stadium, but his standards don't change.

Lane Johnson is another player who will likely be a first-ballot Hall of Fame inductee. Many experts suggest that Lane is the best right tackle in the entire NFL. He followed a unique path to get to this point. He has dominated the NFL tackle position for over a decade, but his athletic prowess hasn't always been on the offensive line. During his early years playing football, he spent time as a quarterback and later as a tight end. The athletic skills necessary to succeed in those positions helped set him up for success when he transitioned to tackle. However, Lane's unwavering dedication to physical preparation may be the key separator in his development.

If you ever get the chance to visit his home in southern New Jersey, you will undoubtedly be given a tour of "the barn," as it has affectionately become known. The barn is a detached building on his property, only a few steps from the main house. As you enter the main area, you are transformed into a weight-lifting paradise. Lane has some equipment that even professional sports teams don't have in their training facilities. He has spent years with his trainer, Gabe Rangel, to create the best and most efficient training atmosphere for when he is at home. He has built a supplemental training program to add to his already rigorous daily training in the Philadelphia Eagles facility. The STANDARD aligns well with the intense approach that Lane takes to his physical preparation. That detailed approach to every aspect of his training and recovery allows him to create an edge over the competition.

Lane's nutrition is another aspect that helps set him apart from others. While hiring a personal chef can be considered easy when you have the monetary resources to do so, the discipline and commitment to not sway from the nutritional regimen is another story. Unfortunately, I have witnessed numerous players who have the necessary resources but still fail because they lack the discipline necessary to build standards in their daily habits.

The players mentioned above have sought ways to apply a personal standard of excellence to their daily routines. This is possible for all of us, no matter what industry we work in and no matter our resources; we all have a choice to make when it comes to following a disciplined approach to our daily standards. While situations change, one thing remains true: we have control over our choices. The responsibility for consistently living up to our personal standards falls upon us. Apply a greater standard to your daily actions and watch as you become a better version of yourself over time. This will not be an overnight process. Instead, as you apply the standard consistently over time, you will gradually build momentum through daily discipline.

Call to Action:
The Standard: Minus Habit and Plus Habit

- Minus Habit
  - I want you to focus and reflect on one unhealthy habit that you will get rid of this month. Commit to getting rid of this habit TODAY!

- Plus Habit
  - Next, commit to one healthy habit that you will add this month. Commit to adding this healthy habit consistently each day to align with and heighten your personal standards. Add this habit TODAY!

As we build winning standards into our daily habits, we develop confidence that positive outcomes are inevitable. We must always be ready to adapt to changing situations, but when we have set high standards in our daily lives, we can trust that our performance will continue to rise. The next step, as explained in the following chapter, is to find congruence, one of the most important aspects of elite performance in any area of life.

CHAPTER 2

Finding Congruence

What is congruence? Congruence occurs when you combine passion and skill. When you find congruence, the work becomes the reward. This allows you to stay in the process of attacking one step at a time. Very often, we think about the long-term outcome.

When we have outcome-based goals, we will often overlook important steps, although not always intentionally. It becomes easier to miss steps because we're too focused on the end of the tunnel. However, when we focus on the process, it's much easier to stay locked into the immediate steps that must be taken at the moment.

Passion separates those who may have a natural skill but lack motivation and commitment. With passion as your fuel, you will put the time and effort into increasing your skill in this area and become a higher-level achiever. This can happen in various areas of life, including sports, business, leadership, family life, and everything in the middle. Clearly, we must possess a basic level of skill in the area to begin with.

Promontory's Passion for Excellence

One example that I love to look at is wine. I'm a huge fan of wine. I've been fortunate to visit Napa Valley multiple times, and one of my favorite places to visit there is the estate at Promontory. This incredible estate offers even more incredible wine. Promontory comes from the Harlan family of wines, which, if you know wine, is one of the most elite producers in the world. Their process for producing wine is a multi-year undertaking. When you talk to the winemaker and the people who work there, you feel the intensity and care as they talk about the process that goes into aging and eventually bringing out the perfect bottle of wine.

Instead of aging between 18 and 24 months like a lot of wineries would choose to do, Promontory ages for four years. Also, instead of barreling the wine in new oak from France, which is very common amongst the elite estates and producers, Promontory chose to use Austrian oak, as it seemed to provide a better medium for aging the wine. Promontory knew it would take several years to get one of these Austrian oak barrels. They come from a unique family that, for several generations, produced them only for their own use.

Promontory soon realized that this would be a ten- to 20-year pursuit. If they were only focused on the end of those ten to 20 years, they would, without a doubt, miss important steps. However, when you focus on the process and take things one day at a time, you will inevitably have a better outcome at the end of the day. So, why does passion matter? Because passion leads to deep care for the details that go into producing this wine.

One of the other aspects that blew me away was hearing stories about when they have cold weather that results in a frost. In Napa Valley, it can get chilly in the evenings, especially during the winter months. If they receive a frost alert, you will see workers scrambling, sometimes at 2 a.m., with extension cords and blow dryers to go out to the grapes and the vines to heat them up. One small frost could be devastating for that year's vintage.

The detail, passion, and multitude of steps that go into making sure each grape is handled with care are inspiring. As you think about this, what aspects of your life do you attack with such passion and care in a relentless pursuit to make them better? That's your first hint that it may be something that can build in congruence. When you carefully cultivate the soil like Promontory does because you care that much about producing the best bottle of wine you possibly can, how can you not be a success?

Imagine if we all took that same passion and applied it to our everyday opportunities, whether we're trying to start a new workout routine or become a better version of ourselves in our current role at work. There are several other examples in the wine industry that we could talk about, but what I love the most is the production. It's not an overnight process. Every winery has years of history. It's incredible to see the passion that winemakers pour into producing the best grape that will lead to a great bottle of wine. This also takes a team effort, and that's the beauty of congruence.

Excelling through Congruence

When you combine skill and passion, it can lead to things like phenomenal wine, and it can also lead to championships in sports and life. Whether you're in sales or another industry, this will lead to a better outcome for you. People with a level of congruency attack the process relentlessly. Special forces are a great example of this; we've heard why the standard makes the Navy SEALs some of the best. They take special after-action reviews to heart. They combine their elite level of skill with demanding preparation. They also love accountability, and they dive into it. The passion they exhibit in extremely difficult training leads them to elite performance.

At our first-ever NFL collaborative player health and safety meetings in 2024, we were fortunate to have General Brian Fenton, head of SOCOM, present to the group. He talked about holding people accountable to create a better outcome for the team. Then he talked about passion. Sometimes, the people who do critical jobs go unseen, unheard, and unthanked. Despite this, they still attack their jobs with a passion and care that sets them apart. This is what special operation units are based on, and it's what every great team that I have ever seen is based on, including in business.

In fact, congruence leads to higher achievement and better outcomes in any industry. Ndamukong Suh is one example of this that pops into mind. As an athlete, he's had a Hall of Fame-caliber career, but I am more impressed by his success as an entrepreneur. This is a person who regularly phones Warren Buffett. He seeks out the best of the best because he cares about learning and growing in everything that he does. When he pours his heart and soul into a new business venture, he goes all in. When he did this on the football field, he also went all in. And when he's on TV or other media outlets, he goes all in. He cares, and he dives in. Suh taps into his passion, finds his congruence, and then takes it one step at a time, relentlessly ensuring that he's doing the right thing each step of the way.

Aaron Donald is another player who comes to mind. In his offseason workouts, he attacked every aspect of his game. You could see his passion and the sweat that he poured into it, and you could also see how he loved every minute of it. This led to his skills improving. He's been genetically blessed, but when you combine that with the passion that it takes to work out three to four hours every single day of the offseason when many of your teammates and opponents are staying at home, sleeping, or vacationing, that leads to an increased level of skill and a better outcome. And it certainly did for him.

I'll never forget one of my favorite stories about AD. It was my first year in Los Angeles when I was working with the Rams. One night, I went back to the facility around 9 p.m. to grab something from my office. As I walked through the dark, empty building, I noticed one small light on in the defensive line room. When I walked by, I poked my head in, and who was in there? It was Aaron Donald, watching film. Why? Because he was trying to get an edge on his opponent. He had already put in a day of physical work. Then, he went home to spend time with his family and play the extremely important role of a father. After his kid's bedtime, he dove right back into his passion! Those consistent habits are part of the reason he is considered one of the best EVER at his position.

To find your own congruence, ask yourself, *What skills do I have, and what am I passionate about?* Whatever the answer is, tap into it. If you do, you'll end up with better outcomes.

Nate Burleson is perhaps one of the best examples of someone who found congruence. Nate had an amazing career in professional football. He played for 11 seasons, had over five thousand career receiving yards, and always had some of the best touchdown celebrations on the team. Nate also has an infectious personality. He commands a room and is a natural-born leader. I was fortunate to spend four years with Nate while we were both with the Detroit Lions. Watching him become one of the most important leaders on the team is something I'll never forget. More impressive were Nate's passion and work ethic as he prepared to transition to another career after he finished playing football.

Nate is now involved with several national television shows and has quickly become a leading network TV personality, he's even a four-time Emmy winner. What people may not know is that Nate worked to hone his craft for decades. When he was in the prime of his playing career, he embraced every opportunity to gain experience on camera. Whether it was optional interviews or attending broadcast boot camps around the country, Nate said yes. He allowed his natural charisma and skill to blend with his passion for entertaining people.

I asked Nate once during his stint with Detroit what he would eventually do when his career was over. Without hesitation, he looked at me and said confidently, "I'm going to be on TV and see where it takes me." He had found congruence. In the years that followed, he continued to develop his skills; he put effort into learning and improving all aspects of hosting and being on camera. He sought ways to increase his camera presence, dove into the details of vocal tones, and worked to master his craft so the viewer would be drawn in by his presence. He worked HARD to become elite, just as he had already done as a professional football player. I'm excited to see where Nate goes next. I'm confident it will be somewhere great because he has already been preparing for it!

Embrace Discomfort

Where did my passion begin? Where did I find my congruence? My passion for physical training and improving performance began years ago. I was in middle school, and my parents gave me a rusty old weight bench that they probably found at a garage sale and some plastic weights filled with sand. I can't remember the exact name on the frame, but I can still recall the feel, the look, the aesthetics. The padding on the bench was worn thin, the rusted hooks held a smaller version of what you would consider a normal barbell. Luckily, I wasn't strong enough to lift heavy weight at that point, otherwise, there is a good chance that the bench would have crumbled. I remember putting the bench and weights in a corner of my bedroom. There, I would crank out sets: bench press, upright rows, bicep curls, bent-over rows, whatever I could do. Back then, all I had access to were muscle and fitness magazines. I would read to gain any knowledge available and then attempt to implement it into my training.

I didn't know it at the time, but I was developing a passion. Once again, when passion meets skill, your congruence starts to develop. So, from that moment on, I learned a couple of things. Number one, grit and determination. It doesn't matter what your equipment is or what your surroundings are. Do we try to build our environment in a way that's going to help with productivity and the ultimate outcome of success? Absolutely, if you have the means, buy the best equipment and get whatever you can. If you don't, there's no excuse. The only thing we're limited by is our imagination, and that goes for everything in life, specifically physical training.

As I developed this passion, I realized from using this garage-sale weight bench that I could make anything work. Fast-forward to later in life, and I'm the head strength and conditioning coach and, later on, the director of strength training performance for the Los Angeles Rams. We were in a very humble facility because they had moved to Los Angeles from St. Louis. In effect, we were operating out of several modular buildings connected together to make up our training facility. We had to repair the floor, and we had roof leaks, even the occasional rattlesnake. Not to mention, the poisonous black widow spiders we would find in various places around the facility. I remember telling the players, "Guys, we need to lean into this. You've got to love this. This is what a gritty team is made of. We are developed in places like this so that we can go out and dominate the teams that are spoiled with all the comforts of a brand new facility. We're going to make this OUR advantage."

Growing up in a small town in Michigan helped me develop the grit that would take me to a Super Bowl with the Los Angeles Rams and then with the Philadelphia Eagles. I knew that the passion was there because it continued to stoke that fire inside of me. Later on, when I got into high school and finally got my driver's license, I joined a gym: Powerhouse Gym in Monroe, Michigan. It would take me about 25 minutes to drive there. My daily schedule was quite simple. I'd wake up early, go to school, go to practice, either football, baseball, or basketball, depending on the time of year it was. Then I would make the drive to the gym and spend a couple of hours there. I'd get home late at night, exhausted. After drinking a protein shake on my way home, I would lay my head down and have no trouble falling asleep.

Those nights are fun to look back at. Spending the dark hours of night grinding, adding in the work, and putting in the time, effort, and dedication that would eventually lead to success. What did that lead me to? Even today, wherever I've lived, I've had to have some kind of fitness equipment at our home. It is usually some form of simple tools. It might be kettlebells, dumbbells, other weights, a TRX strap—whatever allows me to introduce some very uncomfortable challenges when I'm in my own home.

Eventually, I began to see the gains from all the effort that I was putting in. I started to notice changes in my body and the muscle mass I was developing. I was also bench pressing and squatting more weight than my friends. In essence, I had found a cheat code early in life, and that cheat code is hard work through consistency. It's being willing to dive into the work and get as much as you possibly can from it. It's grinding through and then putting in even more effort the next day.

I started running faster. I started jumping higher. I became stronger. I started beating my friends in competitions—and I found joy in that competition. My improvements drove a lot of my teammates to reach higher levels, too, because we fed off of each other. This led me to one of the most important lessons of my life, one I feel every high achiever needs to embrace: you have to learn to enjoy discomfort. You have to be able to get comfortable with being uncomfortable.

A lot of the time, we want to turn away from discomfort. We want to shy away, shut down, pack up, take an easy day, make an excuse. What I learned is that we have to lean into those moments. Whether we like it or not, we will face challenging times. How do we prepare for when those times come? We prepare through repetition. We can introduce these tough times through a workout or a mentally challenging task. I was the person at practice who would throw on an additional weight vest to make it even harder. I was the guy wearing the crazy jump shoes that are supposed to increase your vertical jump. I found whatever ways I could to add discomfort, and then I hustled as much as I possibly could.

If you choose discomfort more often, you will apply the cheat code that leads to success. Laziness is easy, but success is paid for by hard work and discipline through discomfort over the long haul. It takes consistent and relentless work to get to where you want to be. When you lean into that stress, lean into that work, and find ways to challenge yourself, success is right around the corner. But don't worry about that.

Worry about the process. Stay in the moment. Develop that grit. Find the attitude that takes things up a notch and makes what you're doing more challenging. Find your life's pathway to congruence and lean into it.

I challenge you to ask yourself about your passions. I challenge you to tap into them. I challenge you to go deep and to see what you are truly passionate about so you can find your congruence. Then I challenge you to put in the work that it takes to truly become great in that area. Put intentional thought into this exercise and write it down. Repeat this exercise at least twice a year, continue to update your passions, and then attack them with the skills you need to become better at them.

Call to Action:
Congruence

- Why do you do what you do?
    - Write down or type your answer to this question. If you are a coach, why do you coach? If you work in sales, why do you sell? If you are a parent, why are you raising children?

_____

_____

_____

- Next, I challenge you to read this out loud. If you're comfortable enough, read this in front of a group of people.
  - This group could be your immediate family, coworkers, or anyone else you trust to listen.

I've found that doing this exercise in a large group setting is the most powerful way to incorporate it. When you read your statement to others, it allows them to keep you accountable. Surrounding yourself with a room full of people who have a growth mindset will help you tap into your deep-rooted passions. Assess your why and lean into the passions that exist within you. Find YOUR congruence and enjoy the work that surrounds it! Once you have, the next chapter will teach you how to apply one of the key aspects of highly successful people—urgency!

CHAPTER 3

Default Urgent

When making decisions, the power of urgency is one of our most valuable tools. The greatest leaders in the history of our world have operated with a tempo, and that tempo has been set to urgent. I'm not saying that you should dive into things haphazardly. I'm saying there is an urgent attitude held by anyone who becomes a high achiever. This occurs when making decisions, but it's true in many other areas as well. When in doubt, our default setting should be set to urgent.

Simply choosing to take a positive step forward is a powerful tool. The first step is always the most important. Why? Because it creates momentum. Once we build momentum, it is easier to continue. The hardest part is the start. Once we start and build momentum, a one-step-at-a-time approach with urgency becomes a reality, and that is what ultimately leads to positive long-term outcomes.

Urgency is not just about making decisions or taking action. It's about seizing opportunities, including the chance to apologize. Is there someone you need to make amends with? Don't delay. Reach out. Embracing urgency in actions that lead to better outcomes is a powerful tool. It's also about taking ownership and accountability for our actions, a key to personal and professional growth.

Urgent Self-Reflection

Every day, we have the opportunity to reflect on our actions and consider what we could have done better and what we did well. This critical self-reflection, this urgency in looking at ourselves in the mirror, is the key to becoming better versions of ourselves. I've had to embrace this process many times in my NFL career, particularly when it comes to data collection and modifications during training sessions.

As we go into a training session, there are literally millions of rows of data that we can analyze. You could quickly be paralyzed by all of the data and rows and rows of numbers. Appropriate urgency is important in this setting. Once again, there has to be alignment and integration of the data. We must align with monitoring the data and then make the decision that's most appropriate at the time. Do we do this haphazardly? No, we do this with an intentional focus and urgency in our decision making.

As we go through a typical training session, we might have force-plate data pouring in live. The force plate is a device utilized to test several metrics that can give us important information on the neuromuscular fatigue status of each athlete. It is most commonly used with a counter-movement jump exercise. When data comes in, it's critical to analyze it as quickly as possible, as flags might pop up based on asymmetries or where there's a big decline in performance.

Sometimes, you have less than five minutes to decide how many modifications you're going to make in that training session. This later builds into how you will adjust practice and some of the other physical loading of that particular player. When you're doing this for over 90 players in less than an hour, urgency must be your default setting. You also have to look at this when you're monitoring practices and games. Once again, in a typical NFL practice session, you will have endless rows of data thrown at you on a daily basis. How do you look at this? How are you integrating this data into your decision-making as a leader? Urgency comes in all forms and sizes.

You have to be urgent in analyzing the data, and then you have to be urgent with your recognition of the patterns that may lead to a particular injury. Once you have found a pattern, you must urgently decide what you feel is most appropriate for the player at that time. Repetition becomes the next most important variable—the more you do this, the better you will get at it. In life, it is very similar—the more that we can continuously take an urgent step in the right direction, the more often we will have positive outcomes.

Urgency should be our setting at all times. Once again, don't mistake this setting for ignoring the need to assess the situation. There are times when we have to be urgently patient. You have to sit down, take a breath, reset, and then focus on what your next best step will be. This happens all the time in sports, business, and life. Think about your family or social life. Think about the times when you've had to urgently step in or urgently step back. There are times when we have to zoom out and analyze all the things that we have to do. I implore you to do this with an urgent attitude because the better you can do this, the better the outcomes that you will have.

Unexpected Challenges

One of the most important areas in which we can have urgency is dealing with unexpected challenges. The unexpected can pop up in any way, shape, or form. One of my favorite stories about this is from when I was in London with the Detroit Lions in preparation for a game that was part of the International Series that season.

It was 2015. We were not having a good season based on our winning percentage. We were in the midst of a bit of adversity, and we had started very slowly. As we approached the midway point of the season, we had a London game scheduled just before our bye week. Many teams in the NFL will have a travel strategy where they will stay for the entire week to get acclimated and allow your circadian rhythm to adjust to the London time zone. So, we were flying out on a Monday after a home football game that Sunday in Detroit. We also fired multiple coaches that Monday; their bags had already been checked for the evening flight to London. I'll never forget that because some were close friends, and many actually kept the luggage tags from their bags to remind them of just how crazy a business the NFL can be.

So, as they were being escorted out of the building, we were boarding an overnight flight to another country. Since we traveled overnight, by the time we landed, it was Tuesday morning local time. We'd attempted to get adequate sleep on the plane, and now we locked into the local London time zone to begin acclimating our body clocks. Tuesday was our players' day off. As they rested, we had some come in for optional training, and we had others performing recovery work. Then came Wednesday.

Wednesday is a work day in the NFL. It's typically a heavy practice day. You will sometimes have a training session in the morning, hold several meetings throughout the remainder of the morning, have a brief lunch, and then get on the practice field. I'll never forget this one day in the United Kingdom.

When I arrived at the practice field, I started getting ready for my typical duties, like running the stretch for the team. Our equipment manager, Tim O'Neill, approached me and said, "Hey, we're going to get you fitted for your headset, and we'll get you all squared away for this week. You're probably going to be on the cable because, in London, we have to have you attached, and we don't have the wireless mics on the sidelines."

I took a step back, trying to comprehend what Tim was saying. Then I replied, "I apologize, but what the heck are you talking about?"

Timmy looked at me and said, "Oh, no one's told you. You're on the headset. You're helping coach special teams now. With the staff adjustments and the coaches that we've let go, we're short right now. We're going to need you to step in. We're going to need you to help and assist with special teams."

The urgency that set into my head at that moment was palpable. Usually, in situations like this, you realize: *All right, I have two options. I can just kind of roll with this, or I can jump into this with some urgency.* When your default setting is stuck on urgent, you have no option. You dive in and attack the situation because it's the only thing to do. So, at that moment, I made a decision. I said, "Okay, I'm going to dive into these meetings and learn everything that I can." A lot of it was based on personnel packages and adjustments there, and the other part was learning the scheme and anything else that I should know. This also was a default urgent action because it's not like I gave up the role that I currently held, which was the assistant strength and conditioning coach. At the time, we only had two full-time strength and conditioning coaches. So, as I stayed within my normal day-to-day roles, which were obviously heavy, I also dove into this additional role. If my default setting had not been one of urgency, in no way, shape, or form would I have had an opportunity to be successful in that transition. But I dove in and soaked up as much knowledge as I possibly could.

I asked myself, *What do I need to do? What do I need to get ahead of?* That default urgent setting allowed me to look forward and say, "Okay, what can I control right now on Wednesday that will lead me to a better outcome once we get to Sunday in London against our opponent?" That default urgent setting allowed me to minimize the mistakes. Were there some? Absolutely. Are there always growing pains? Yes. Once again, we learn, and we fail forward, and that's an urgent action in and of itself. Default urgency needs to be our setting, especially when we make mistakes. Get up, take that next step forward, and build momentum immediately.

Reflecting back, we finished that season on a positive note, and we actually turned it around. We won several games in the second half of the season and showed that we could demonstrate and live with the urgent resilience required when you face any form of adversity.

It was a crazy time but an immensely valuable learning experience, one that led to great growth and adaptability. It made me realize how important urgency is, and it allowed me to attack other steps and processes with my default setting stuck on urgent, helping me achieve other things in sports, business, and life.

Attacking the Problem with Urgency

Another time when the unexpected struck was in Los Angeles when I was coaching with the Rams. We had multiple wildfires each year that we lived there. One of the worst years was in 2018. At the time, unfortunately, it was the deadliest wildfire season in the history of the state of California, but I believe that it has since been surpassed. During this particular wildfire, we were scheduled for a game in Mexico City, which meant that we would have to be physically prepared to compete at a high altitude. To do this, we planned to take the team to Colorado. Why Colorado? Because it was as close as we could get to the elevation of Mexico City while we were still stateside. Also, we could train at the Air Force Academy and use the United States Olympic Committee facilities for some of our other training. We planned this far in advance, almost a full year ahead of time.

As we approached the scheduled trip to Colorado, the wildfires started, and we had to change multiple practice days and adjust our schedule. We even had to move our team and our families into a hotel before a home game the week before we were to leave for Colorado. However, in situations like this, you adapt and attack with urgency. You control the things that you can control, and you try to minimize the impact of things that you might not be able to control.

The night before our scheduled departure, the wildfires got worse. And the next day, when we left for Colorado, the fires continued to spread. It was a crazy time in California. To add to the stressful environment, a local shooting had taken place in a restaurant right by our training facility in Thousand Oaks, California; numerous people had lost their lives. Amidst all this chaos, the organization, in particular Stan Kroenke, who owned the team, committed to chartering a separate plane because several families and members of our organization had been forced out of their homes through mandatory evacuation. Mr. Kroenke covered the financial cost of flying our families to Colorado so we could be safely together. This was a moment of surprise, but did we attack it with urgency? Yes, the organization handled it extremely well.

I wish I could say that the unexpected stopped there. We were scheduled to leave for Mexico later that week. Then we got a call from our field maintenance crew. These are members of the organization who specialize in turf and field management. They were in Mexico, and after pulling up the sod on the game field, they didn't think we could safely play on it.

This was Thursday night. We were at the Air Force Academy, concluding a practice session. Once they showed us video of the field on FaceTime, we gathered that it was definitely in no shape to play. It would unnecessarily put our players in harm's way. Since we care about player safety and health, we attacked the problem. This was another unexpected event, and we attacked it with urgency.

We said, "What do we have to do?" We informed the proper team officials and started having conversations within the league circles about how we would move the game back to California. About 48 hours later, we moved the game back to the LA Coliseum, and it turned into a Monday night game against the Kansas City Chiefs.

This game was one of the most memorable I've ever been a part of. The organization offered all the tickets for free to first responders who were impacted by the local shooting and the wildfires. The atmosphere during the game was incredible. After being a part of other big games, including the Super Bowl, this one still sticks out in my mind as one of the most memorable of my career. It was a shootout, and the final score was 54 to 51. We were fortunate to come away with the win. Patrick Mahomes and Jared Goff were on fire, and our defense made huge plays at the end, including an extremely important defensive touchdown by Samson Ebukam. Even more notable was the emotion that you could feel inside that stadium.

What I'll always remember and reflect upon is how we urgently adapted during unexpected times. Multiple things were thrown at us that week, and our response led to success, not just in that game but within the culture. Later that season, we were fortunate to have a playoff berth, and we eventually made it to the Super Bowl. We made this happen because, in part, of how close our team became. Though we handled the unexpected with urgency, we also connected and formed stronger bonds.

This experience is a great example of how the unexpected can become the ultimate weapon for us. When we attack the unexpected with urgency, discipline, and intentional focus on the details and the actions that we must take to find the outcome that we're looking for, good things will happen. We did this in this situation.

Another unexpected situation happened when I was in Miami, working with the Dolphins, and the team was evacuated because of an incoming hurricane. This forced us to adjust the team's schedule and training. Fortunately, we did not have to move the game that week, but it's another example of having to adapt and adjust when the unexpected happens.

What's an even better example of adapting to the unexpected? The pandemic we all just experienced in 2020. The NFL schedule was played out, but many adjustments had to be made. Every day, we tried to learn to expect the unexpected and then attack with urgency whatever we could control. Now, as we adapt and adjust to life, learning from those lessons will help us be better the next time the unexpected pops up. We don't have to fear the unexpected; we just have to attack with urgency and with purpose those things that we can control.

Urgent Adaptability

Urgent adaptability is a necessity in leadership and life, making us better versions of ourselves. It won't always be perfect, and we will make mistakes, but taking urgent action to step back before you take your next step forward so you can create positive momentum will help. We must have urgency in action.

The tempo of our actions will dictate the results that we get both now and later. How do you train for urgency? In the NFL, when you have 90 players on a field, and you're trying to decipher all the information and data coming in, you have to do so with urgency. The decision has to be made in a split second. You live and die by those decisions, and then you learn from them when they're the wrong ones. After the decision has been made, how quickly do you begin the actual work? This is one of the most important aspects of urgency.

What are you waiting for? Are you overanalyzing your decision? This can happen in work, in any industry. While it's important to step back, recognize your emotions, and consider all the things that your decision may impact, it's also important to take that necessary step. Try not to be paralyzed by the analysis. Instead, allow yourself to step forward with a default urgent setting.

I always challenge people to wake up with urgency. Why? Because it becomes your first win of the day. If you have urgency when you wake up, you will have urgency throughout the day. This will also allow you to start your day with a win. If you hit snooze, to me, that's the first loss of the day.

Some days, however, we need to rest. This is absolutely fine and also very much encouraged. However, when it's a day that you know you need to wake up, whether it's to get a workout in, get to work at your place of employment, take the kids to school, or countless other tasks, what are you doing to urgently wake up, get out of bed, and take that first step forward? Remember, the first step is the most important because it will create momentum for the rest of the day!

What areas do you need to apply enhanced urgency to? Do you have urgency in working out? Are you urgently taking care of yourself physically? You have to have urgency in taking care of yourself so you can attack the day and take care of others who depend on you to show up. Urgency in working out and urgency in your nutritional habits will lead to long-term health and success in your life and the lives of others. Are you setting out to be the urgent example for the people in your life, whether they are the people you lead at work or your family, children, or spouse? If you're saying to yourself that you don't lead anyone, I challenge you to recognize the fact that you lead YOURSELF each and every day.

Urgent Grace

One area that's often not talked about is the need for urgent grace when dealing with others. We are emotional humans. We experience a variety of emotions every single day. When you understand that you have to have urgent grace when dealing with others, you can separate from the emotions that sometimes run rampant when you encounter conflict. Allowing yourself to act rashly before you urgently assess your personal emotions will usually only lead to further conflict.

Conflict resolution is one of the hardest things to figure out. You have to find empathy and apply grace in your relationships, both with the people you interact with at work and in your social circles. There is a difference between applying grace to a situation and allowing others to walk all over you. We should all have basic principles and standards of living that are non-negotiable. We expect to be treated with the basic level of respect that all human beings deserve. Don't make the mistake of offering grace when something fundamentally wrong has occurred. It is only necessary in those small moments when someone simply makes a mistake. Rather than completely overreacting because someone left a light on in the house, apply urgent grace in this situation. It takes practice, but I promise you that as you gain repetitions in this area, it will lead to less stress and an ability to see past small things that might otherwise have led to further conflict.

I often hear the phrase, "This is a people business." Well, this is a person-to-person life. I firmly believe that. We interact with people on a daily basis. Amongst other things, if you don't have a lot of people around you in your life right now, you interact with yourself. So, how urgent are you with your self-talk? How urgent are you attacking grace when you make a mistake? And how urgent are you when it comes to taking the necessary action steps to fix it? Find empathy and grace in your relationships with others and yourself.

You must also learn from the past with urgency. Kevin Eastman has spent over 40 years working in high-level collegiate and professional basketball. I love what Kevin says in his book *Why the Best Are the Best*: "Learn from the past, produce in the present, and prepare for the future." We actually posted this graphic in the L.A. Rams' weight room, and we attempted to learn from it and live by it every day.

I always love to say that there is a reason that our rearview mirror is much smaller than our front windshield. The rearview mirror is still necessary, and it is okay to occasionally sneak a peek, but I never want to trip on something that's behind me. I never want to stumble because of something from my past. We must learn from the past, and then we must attack forward. We must urgently take that step forward because our view through the windshield will take us where we're going to go. Keep your eyes on the windshield. Don't hesitate to look back so that you can learn with urgency from our past, but make sure that we're not dwelling on it.

I will issue a warning here because I firmly believe that repetitious grace for the same mistakes equals enablement. If you are continuously giving yourself grace for the same mistakes, you are enabling your negative actions. Have you made the same mistake seven days in a row this week? Have you skipped your workout? Have you hit the snooze button multiple times every day? If so, then your action needs to be more urgent. You need to change the behavior, and you need to change it immediately. Take action with the default setting of urgency and apply it to your daily habits. This will lead to better outcomes.

We are our daily habits. Do your daily habits align with your goals? This is a simple question, but it's not easy to answer because, sometimes, we have to take a critical look in the mirror, and then we have to take that next step forward. We must give ourselves grace, but not so much that we continue to make the same mistakes. Identify the things that are within your control to change. This is another action that must have urgency attached to it. When we identify things that are within our control, it allows us to focus. If you cannot control a certain circumstance, it doesn't do you a lot of good to worry about it. Once again, that's like looking in the rearview mirror. Allow yourself to step forward with urgency on the things that you can control. This will also stop negative emotions from hijacking your thoughts.

Once you identify the things that you can control, next, you have to prioritize the most important thing and then get to work with urgency. We have to prioritize, and then we have to combine an urgent attitude with a positive step forward for improved outcomes. I love the Serenity Prayer because it reminds me of this. It goes, "God, grant me the serenity to accept the things I cannot change, the courage to change the things that I can, and the wisdom to know the difference." If you apply urgency to this, it will put you on the path to accomplishing your future goals.

Flamingo

What does a flamingo have in common with urgency? In our family, the word "flamingo" is nearly synonymous with urgency. I'm still not sure why we landed on this word, but it has become a staple in the Rath household. When any member of our family says, "FLAMINGO," urgency appears like a magical and invisible powder that overtakes the rest of the family.

The basic flamingo rules are simple. Once a family member has declared that it is time for a flamingo, the entire family gathers in our living room and takes a seat in our predetermined spots on the sofas and chairs. The family member who called the flamingo then takes center stage. The first and most important rule is that everyone else stops everything that they are doing and gives full and undivided attention to the flamingo-calling individual. This means no phones, tablets, or toys of any kind. We keep eye contact with the person speaking, and only one person speaks at a time.

This has become a sacred time in our home. The flamingo has been used for a wide variety of purposes. Some of the more common ones revolve around a certain member of the family who wishes to apologize for a mistake or outburst. I can humbly admit that I have called my fair share of flamingos. As we have embraced this family tradition, I have also witnessed our children use this tool for other tactics. One example is when our youngest daughter, Emmy, called a flamingo because she had secretly worked to create a personal handwritten note for each member of the family. This has led to many incredible moments that I will always remember. The main component of these impactful moments is urgency. When we hear the word "flamingo," we all come together with an urgent attitude. This intentional urgency creates a place where impactful lessons can be shared.

Urgency is one of the most important lessons we can learn, and we can add urgency to our daily lives in various ways. Think about the example you are leaving for those whom you lead. Do your daily actions demonstrate the importance of taking urgent action with the things that you can control? When you choose to harness the power or urgency, immense personal growth becomes possible.

Call to Action:
Urgency: The Daily Toe Test

- The Daily Toe Test is simple, but sometimes, it's not easy.
    - The daily toe test is a challenge to every one of us. How fast can we get out of bed when our alarm clock goes off in the morning? The first challenge is to never hit the snooze button, no matter how tempting.
    - The next step is to get your feet on the ground before you hear that second beep.
    - How fast can you urgently get out of bed? And how often do you do this? This is the first of many victories that await you every day.
    - I will issue a warning. This can scare the family pet that sleeps in your bed, or your spouse, or children if they've meandered into your bedroom. So, do this with caution but do it with urgency.

As we learn to apply greater urgency to our actions, the next step is to learn the art of zoomability. The next chapter will lead you through the process of zooming in and out consistently to gain a better understanding of every situation that you find yourself in.

CHAPTER 4

Telescope to Microscope: How to Refocus with Zoomability

What is zoomability? It's a practice that everyone in a leadership position—but also anyone who deals with people—must aim to master if they want to become a better communicator and collaborator. As we wind through this world of emotions, we have to be able to zoom in and out to separate from the emotions that sometimes cause us to have negative reactions to various daily situations that we encounter.

Conflict resolution is one of the most important things that we can all improve on. Even if you consider yourself good at it, no one is good enough. Zoomability allows us to zoom out to a 30,000-foot view and then rapidly zoom right back into a microscopic view. As we zoom out, I challenge you to detach from yourself, separate from your emotions, and allow yourself to see the situation from a higher vantage point so you can actually see the entire landscape.

Visualize the Zoom

Zoomability, as we touched on in the previous chapter, requires urgency. One method that can help you put this into practice is to visualize how you will zoom out. View your current situation as if you are a filmmaker holding a video camera. Your goal is to capture the entire scene. What is happening in the corner of the room that you otherwise would not have noticed? Is there a storyline taking shape based on someone's body language? Slow down and scan the room so you can capture the entire scene.

Once you learn to do this, and this happens with repetition, you will learn to see the full environment. How many people are you dealing with? How are they reacting? What are their emotions? What is their body language telling you? How are they responding to your body language? How are your tone and attitude impacting the situation? This is a very important aspect. The more you practice this, the better you will become at understanding how you're reacting to certain situations.

Are you reacting negatively because of someone else's tone of voice? Well, you can control your body language. Zoom out. I challenge you to look at yourself and how your actions and reactions impact others with whom you are communicating. I've made several mistakes in this area. I realized in certain situations that the intensity with which I spoke created more friction in the conversation than I had intended. How you say something is just as important as what is being said. This is often the problem with electronic communication, such as text messages and emails. Many times, people assume a specific tone within the text, and unfortunately, our natural tendency is to assume that the tone is negative toward us.

As you zoom out and zoom back in, you should feel yourself resetting and then refocusing on a more advantageous way to move forward. Once you learn to do this, zooming back in becomes the easy part. That's you controlling your actions. I challenge everyone to practice the zoom-out much more than they do the zoom-in when they are first trying to get used to this method.

Zooming With Urgency

As you zoom out, you start to see things that you otherwise would have been blind to. You understand your surroundings and how your decisions impact others. When you do this with intentionality and urgency, you can detach from not only your emotions but also those of others. Ultimately, when we make bad decisions, it's typically due to emotions. Our ability to zoom in and zoom out will help us make clear decisions for our team and current situation.

If you are in a team setting and you're leading numerous people, I challenge you to make this a common practice. This happens all the time in sports, particularly when it comes to making international travel decisions. If you're taking the team to a place like London, you have to zoom out to see how this will impact the culture and organization.

You also have to be able to rapidly zoom into each player and how it will impact their personal performance. As you do, you will need to zoom in and out in multiple ways. For instance, when we were in California, and I was working for the Los Angeles Rams, we played games in the United Kingdom in multiple seasons. As we did this, several factors had to be considered. One of the most important factors was sleep.

First, we try to maximize our sleep recovery by going to an East Coast city after we play a game and staying there for at least a few days before making the trip to London. This allows us to shift our circadian rhythm to East Coast time, which will make the adjustment to London that much easier. It also allows us to stay within the United States, so we have access to nutritional products and other things that our players have become accustomed to. This is important because the food is sometimes vastly different from what many of our players and staff are used to. It's tough to fuel our team when simple items like ketchup or mustard are not available unless we ship them over months in advance of our trip. The energy and nutrients that an athlete needs to participate in training and a highly competitive football game that lasts for at least 60 minutes are critical variables that will impact their performance. These small details require us to continuously zoom in and out to see the layers of context that could make the difference between winning and losing.

We also look at ways to mitigate general fatigue. First, we try to get adequate sleep on the overnight flight to London. Typically, we depart the East Coast late at night, and some players may choose to supplement things like melatonin to encourage restful, deep sleep. We also give them sleep masks and earplugs so they can shut out light and noise. We even partnered with Bose and offered every player a pair of noise-canceling sleep buds in preparation for a London trip. These are some of the small issues that you have to zoom out to a global view to see. Sleep is important not only for players but also for zooming out even further. How's the coaching staff sleeping? How will we set up the front office personnel in the hotel to maximize their ability to complete their daily work as seamlessly as possible?

Another key aspect is that when we land in London, it's going to be daylight. We want vitamin D at this point, so we want our players to get exposed to it. One of the things that we have is a caffeine station. We've literally had tables set up for when we arrived in London, covered with double shots of espresso for our players and staff. This is one way to encourage them to stay awake because the worst thing that you can do when you're traveling internationally overnight is fall asleep once you get to your destination. We're trying our best to adjust our circadian rhythms to the local time zone quickly.

Once we land, we have to adjust as efficiently as possible. The caffeine allows us to keep players from going to their rooms because we send them directly through the caffeine station. Soon after, we typically do a dynamic movement series with the players. The goal of this is not to induce fatigue or even create a full sweat. The goal is to get them moving outdoors while exposed to direct sunlight, to allow the increase in vitamin D levels, and to let the caffeine begin to take effect.

Next, we zoom out and ask ourselves, "What is the next most important thing to do?" We have to stay on our regular rhythm and schedule. The NFL calendar is very detailed and specific. We have six days to perform everything that we need for next Sunday's competition. As we do, we zoom into the details once again. Each meeting is critical.

Each practice session is critical. Every minute of every walkthrough is critical. So, we send the players to their normally scheduled meetings, still not setting a time to check into our hotel rooms because we don't want to allow someone to accidentally fall asleep during this important early window of adjustment for our bodies.

After the meetings, we take them back to the field and have a walkthrough session. Once again, the goal is to get the players outside and exposed to the sunlight so they can continue to receive natural vitamin D and the caffeine can continue to work. Once the session is over, we take them back inside for a pre-practice lunch to allow for optimal nutrient fueling. Then we get them moving again with a light walk. Often, we set this up by having a locker room located where players have to walk or bike to it. This keeps them on their feet so they can continue to shift their circadian rhythms.

As we're still zoomed out on the team, now we have to zoom back in on each athlete. This is where the minute details take on an even bigger role. As we zoom back in, we start talking about things like each player's pre-practice nutritional strategy. How do we supplement what they're typically used to? Once we're in another country, some foods won't be available. We ship our chefs and nutritionists over well in advance, months before the game is even played, so they can get on the same page and adequately adjust whatever nutritional implementations that we need for that specific week.

We work closely with the hotel staff, particularly the chefs and food service staff. This allows us to zoom back in rapidly so each player can maximize their performance opportunity. Once we do this, we can zoom right back out and say, "Globally, what else do we need to consider? How are we going to adjust our equipment? What if we don't have certain things available?" Then it's time to zoom back into each position coach. Within your coaching staff, you typically have multiple coaches that manage each position. Planning the details around the timing and operation for each coach during practice must be addressed. How well we adapt in a foreign country can have a great impact on the outcome of the game.

Next, we zoom back into the actual adjustments and adaptations that we have to make for that practice session. Another area we will start to look at is how we track these practice sessions. Every step that a player takes is tracked. We typically do this with either a GPS version of a tracker or an RFID, which is a radio frequency version that allows us to track metrics such as player speed, overall distance, accelerations, decelerations, and a host of other metrics. This is a very important aspect of player performance in professional and collegiate sports.

We use these various forms of technology to give us up-to-the-minute data on how far our players are traveling, how fast they're moving, their accelerations, their decelerations, and their changes of direction. This allows us to collect important information so we can make actionable decisions and any modifications that may be necessary for that training session or the remainder of the week. When traveling to London, we don't have access to our in-house RFID system because it is hardwired into the facility back home, so we must zoom out and adapt. We switch to a GPS version of the technology.

Another detail that must be considered is how the data will change due to differing technologies. We must create a comparison report that allows us to compare our historical data to live tracking while overseas. This must all be considered and performed months prior to flying into Europe and getting on the field.

Next, we zoom back into the individual player when we're analyzing this data. We use subjective wellness questionnaires to follow up on levels of soreness, sleep, and stress. Did they not get any sleep on the flight? All right, what is their typical workload? Where are they at right now? What modifications and adjustments do we need to make? These are only a few of the considerations that go into an international game. Improving your ability to zoom in and out is absolutely necessary in this example, and it is also necessary in all of our daily lives.

A zoom-in and zoom-out mentality requires urgency, and this is true every single minute of every single day. The more you practice this, the easier it becomes. There are many things that we have to zoom in and zoom out on in our daily lives. This is also true for every corporation in the United States. There's a dichotomy between the microscopic and telescopic views. Don't think of this as a perfect balance. Sometimes, we get caught up in trying to make everything a perfect 50-50 split. This won't happen, so I challenge you to look at this as an integration instead. Understand that there will be moments when you will need to continuously pivot back and forth between zooming in and out. There are times when you have to zoom out much more frequently than you have to zoom in. If you are dealing with a large number of people, you will have to zoom out the majority of the time.

When you do have to zoom in, I challenge you to use urgency. Apply it, zoom back into the situation, and then try to get back out to see how that situation has changed.

Envisioning the Future

The other thing we can do is allow ourselves to see a little bit in the future. As you zoom out, you can ask yourself, *If I make this decision or adjustment, how will it impact the team? How will it impact me?* Use the zoom-out feature to do that as rapidly as possible, and then zoom back into yourself and the critical decision that you may have to make. This can happen with big and small decisions. It happens to me every day when raising children, and it has happened throughout my entire career. When you take this immediate action, make sure you step back. You have to master this technique of zooming in and out continuously if you want to become a better version of yourself. Allow yourself to see the situation from a higher vantage point by taking a deep breath. Give yourself a brief moment of rest.

One of the most important areas in which we must learn to use the skill of zoomability is with our own excuses. We all have an ego—we are humans, after all, and it's okay to admit that. I have an ego, and you have an ego; once we honestly recognize this, we can take the next step and learn to recognize when it gets in our way. Our excuses tend to correspond with times when we allow our ego to get out of control. If you're thinking to yourself that this never happens to you, say hello to your ego for me because it's right beside you, reading this sentence! When you assess a situation in which you failed or didn't achieve a desired outcome, how do you look back and analyze the scenario? Is your first instinct to blame others and see everything from your own perspective? If so, congratulations; you are just like 99.99% of the world. Our ego distracts us from seeing a situation from other people's perspectives because it is preoccupied with how things impact us directly.

By learning how to zoom out, we can gain better control of the natural tendency to stay locked into our own perspective, where our ego wants to blame others for the failures at hand. By rapidly zooming out and seeing the situation from a telescopic view, we can see various viewpoints. This is critically important if we want to become better at removing our ego and, therefore, limiting the excuses we allow ourselves to make. It is easy to make excuses when you are trapped in your own viewpoint. You see everything through a very personal lens, and your thoughts are controlled by emotion. Zooming out gives you control over those emotions and makes it possible to see the situation through the lenses of others who are involved.

Think about a recent situation in which you allowed yourself to make excuses for why the desired outcome wasn't achieved. Now go back to that time and replay the scenario. However, this time, zoom out first. Look at the entirety of the scenario and see it through the lenses of the other people involved. How could they have seen the situation differently than you? How could they see some of your decisions and actions that could create friction? Was your tone of voice a little aggressive? Did your body language demonstrate a dismissive attitude toward a coworker? As you work through this scenario, see it from a different perspective and rework the situation. How could the outcome improve if you approached a few things differently? Remove your ego, zoom out, and find the perspectives that you need to view!

Just taking a simple breath will allow you to see the situation with a bit more clarity. Then, once again, ask yourself, *How will my next steps impact the team?* Use this global telescope to dictate your vantage point. Then, when necessary, zoom back into each person your decision will impact. How does this decision impact your immediate situation, and then how does it impact the team's? The other thing I love about zoomability is that you have a plan, but adaptability is always welcome. Zooming out can allow you to test specific scenarios and think through potential outcomes.

You have to be able to adapt, and zooming in and zooming out consistently will allow you to do so when necessary. As you do, using the power of zoomability when making key decisions will become a very natural process. The more you do it, the better you will become at it. I challenge you to zoom in and out to create a positive and negative habit list. Do you zoom out, remove your personal bias, and see daily habits from an assessment point of view? How do you grade yourself every day? Zoom out and ask yourself honestly, *How did I perform today?* This can take place at the end of the day. This could take place at the end of a meeting. This could take place at the end of a practice session. We're only limited by our imagination. So, I challenge you: get into the practice of zooming out, reassess how you did, and give yourself a simple grade on a scale of one to ten. How did you do? How did you show up?

Now zoom back into the changes that you can make from a microscopic view. There may be changes that could help the current situation, or you may just have to learn and try to improve the next time that you're in that same situation. But zooming out will allow you to remove your personal bias due to emotions and to see the habits and decisions that you made and how they impacted you and your team. Continue to grade yourself with a humble authenticity. As you zoom back in, consider the decisions that you can change and the actions that you could do a little bit differently from a microscopic point of view. This will allow you to make a better decision the next time.

Pallacanestro Trieste

A great example of an organization successfully implementing zoomability is Pallacanestro Trieste. Trieste is a beautiful town in northeastern Italy. It sits on a narrow strip of land on the Adriatic Sea, borders Slovenia, and is also close to Croatia. You might be curious as to how a professional basketball team in Italy can teach us the art of zooming in and out. It begins with a group of professional students from Wharton's prestigious business school.

This group began the process of acquiring the majority stake in the team in 2022. As the deal was finalized, Trieste was in the midst of their season, playing in the highest level of professional basketball in Italy, "Serie A." While it was a very exciting time for the founding board members and additional investors (myself included), the season began to slowly unravel. With heartbreaking losses and key players missing playing time, the season ended in disappointment. As a result, the team was relegated to a lower level, "Serie A2," for the following season.

For an American investment group, taking control of an organization based on another continent was no easy task. On top of the seemingly endless tasks of building a professional sports organization, learning the customs of another country held its own significant challenges. Building a relationship with local government agencies became paramount as the group worked to integrate into the local culture. This slow and methodical process took time, and it also took the ability to zoom in and out continuously.

As with any professional sports organization, you must maintain a short- and long-term view at all times. What is best for the team at the moment must align with future goals as well. It is extremely difficult to find this balance because the temptation to sacrifice for immediate success is always knocking at the door. The group had some very difficult decisions to make heading into the 2023–2024 season. After suffering the embarrassment of relegation to the lower level of competition, the focus shifted to the leadership of the team. This required an immediate shift in zooming out to see the organization as a whole.

The first order of business was to hire an experienced general manager who could serve as the "CEO" of the organization. The team found their leader in Michael Arcieri. With an impressive resume that combined NBA and Italian front office experience, Trieste made the hire after a deep vetting process. The unique thing about Arcieri accepting the position is that he was in a general manager position for a Serie A team at the time. He chose to take on the challenge of bringing Trieste back to the top league because his wife has family in the Trieste area. Talk about a DEFAULT URGENT decision based on CONGRUENCY for the new general manager.

The focus quickly shifted to zooming back in on the players on the roster. The team had to find the next leader who could create a dynamic and championship-level culture within the locker room. They needed a head coach who could bring a team of individuals together to accomplish the goal of winning a championship. After another extensive vetting process, the team zeroed in on their target. Jamion Christian was hired as the head coach before the 2023–2024 season. Christian, who is also American, brought extensive experience as a head coach at the college level. This would be his first job coaching on the professional level; it would also require a move across the world for the new coach, who had a young family to consider. It was critical for the ownership group to continuously zoom in and out as they chose these two key leaders who would, hopefully, lead the team to a successful return to the highest league by building a winning culture.

As the next season began, the new head coach and general manager worked hard to put the right people in positions to succeed. Leadership requires a constant ability to see the microscopic details that can help you win a game, but at the same time, you must carry a telescope that allows you to see the impact that your decisions will have on the overall organization, both now and in the future. The season had its share of amazing victories and also heartbreaking defeats. The players continued to buy into the new culture that was being developed through intentional daily efforts. There were times when zooming into the details of in-game strategy and tactics was necessary. There were other times when the staff and players had to zoom out to the bigger picture of building sustainable success. As the playoffs approached, the team had suffered a few tough losses.

One of the great costs of leadership is repetition. This requires that a leader demonstrate the standard through their daily efforts, especially during times of adversity. In professional sports, this happens most often when you suffer a loss. The standard must not waver just because the result of a game or string of games wasn't what you had hoped for. In fact, this is when you must double down on your process, and that process must include zoomability.

During the playoffs, the team hit their stride. As the wins piled up, the focus shifted from zooming into the opponent's tendencies and then back out to managing a roster that would sustain elite performance all the way through the final series. As the zooming continued, so did the wins. Trieste found itself in the final series against a tough Cantu team. In a five-game series, Trieste would play the first two games on the road. The team traveled to Cantu, located just outside of Lake Como.

Cantu had an impressive roster; their players were also much bigger than Trieste's. The average height and weight of their players offered Cantu a distinct advantage over the smaller Trieste roster. However, Trieste took Cantu by surprise and controlled the first two games as the visiting team. This brought the series back to Trieste with a potential series-clinching game three in front of their home crowd.

The crowd was on fire in the team's home arena, especially during a season in which a home attendance record was broken. The team and city were ready to clinch this series and earn promotion back into the top league. What a storybook ending, right?

Unfortunately, as the clock ticked down during a well-fought game three, Trieste found themselves down 74–73 with only seconds left. Cantu missed a couple of clutch free throws that would have put the game out of hand. Trieste hit a huge shot to make it a one-shot game with 22 seconds remaining. There was still a chance, and the crowd was electric!

With less than ten seconds remaining, Trieste took possession and drove the floor. They took multiple shots that rattled out, and as one final loose ball bounced toward the sideline, players from both teams strained to gain possession. The ball rolled out of bounds with 1.3 seconds left, and the crowd anxiously awaited the official's signal of possession. When the official pointed in favor of Trieste, the crowd roared. Trieste had a sideline inbound and one last chance to send the arena into an explosion of cheers. With a great screen and an aggressive cut by one of the players, they had an open jump shot for the win… CLANG. BUZZZZZZZ. The two sounds silenced the rowdy crowd. Cantu's small faction of fans, sitting in the isolated and protected section reserved for the other team's support, offered the only noise in the arena. Trieste had a choice to make.

In such moments, it is easy to zoom into the pain of the situation. The team could have said to themselves, "Why didn't we hit the shot? Why didn't we get that one call?" The following day was a rest day, so they had time to think, which can be dangerous if you allow the mind to wander toward the negative side of a situation. In moments like these, we look to our leaders to set the tone through their actions. This allows everyone to lead themselves into the right thought process, which will allow them to attack the situation as an opportunity rather than an obstacle. Zoom out and see the entire picture.

Trieste was still at home for their next game, and they had the support of one of the best crowds in all of Italian basketball. They had controlled games one and two. The size disadvantage had taken them by surprise in game three, specifically in terms of rebounding. With a telescope in one hand and a microscope in the other, the team was ready to learn from their failure and use it to their advantage in game four. They did just that, and two nights later, they dominated Cantu en route to a commanding home victory and CHAMPIONSHIP. The entire city showed up to support the team, which had just used the art of zoomability to earn their promotion back to the top league for the following season.

A lot of lessons can be learned from this team. As I stood on the court next to my wife, watching the confetti fall overhead, I reflected on the efforts and actions that combined to make that moment possible. The next time you are sitting in the midst of victory or defeat, I urge you to zoom out. Allow yourself to remove the emotions that will gladly distract you if you allow them. These emotions will steal one of the greatest gifts available in any situation of triumph or defeat—the gift of LEARNING. Zoom out and zoom in to MOVE FORWARD!

Call to Action
Refocus Exercise

- Think of a moment when you performed at your best. This should be a time when you were in a flow state. Write it down. When was it? Where was it?
  - Next, write down at least two healthy habits that you consistently applied during that time. Give this intentional thought. Be very specific. Were you waking up early during that time?

  Did you have a daily exercise routine? Were you reading each morning? Were you listening to a specific podcast? Be as specific as possible. It could have been having a weekly phone call with a mentor. Write down these two healthy habits and keep them somewhere you can revisit them.

  _____

  _____

  _____

- Now, think of a time when you may have struggled. Consider your surroundings at that time. Zoom out, put yourself back into that situation, and see it from a higher point of view. This could be a work performance, it could be a performance at home, or it could be a time that you were in a social setting.

- o Now, I want you to write down at least two unhealthy habits that were consistently present during that time when you struggled. Once again, be authentic and specific. When was that time? What were those actions? What were the unhealthy habits that were consistently present?

    _____

    _____

    _____

    _____

- TIME FOR ACTION. Now it's time for the most important part of this exercise: use the power of zoomability to refocus your habits. I urge you to learn from these two times and apply the healthy habits that helped you get into the flow state. Be very specific, honest, and authentic. Then, edit out the unhealthy habits.

Edit out the unhealthy habits that you know reduce your performance. If you continue to do these habits and allow them to dominate your day-to-day life, they will limit your overall performance and the outcomes you expect to have later in life. As you apply the healthy habits and edit out the unhealthy ones, watch your performance soar and your day-to-day impact rise. Move forward, attack the process, and use zoomability to refocus your habits every day.

As we move forward, we will apply the power of zoomability to approach new situations with the tools that will lead us to success. One of those tools is humility, and the next chapter explores how maintaining a humble attitude will expand the impact we have on everyone who depends on us.

CHAPTER 5

The Humility Habit

Acts of humility are never limited by our title, our position in life, our role at work, or the name we have. They can be done in any way, shape, or form throughout our daily lives. Acts of humility are the tools that can lead to improved lives for us and those who we choose to impact with them.

We see stories of people displaying humility every single day. I could go through a list of thousands of moments that offer great examples. I could tell you about the time Kevin Demoff, the president of the Los Angeles Rams, gave his hotel room weekly to a low-level staff member or an intern. His room would typically be one of the nicest suites in the hotel when we traveled, and this simple act of humility, giving the room to a young professional starting their career, no doubt made that person's day, week, month, and sometimes year. I could talk to you about Calvin Johnson's daily humility and how he would give access through his Nike account to staff members and support staff who didn't make a lot of money. He made their days by allowing them to get free Nike products that they otherwise couldn't afford.

I could tell you about players in the NFL who give money to support staff at Christmas and other holidays, sometimes tens of thousands of dollars, literally life-changing money for some of these people. I could tell you about players banding together when they heard a staff member or intern had a car break down and buying that person a new vehicle. I could tell you about the time Jim Schwartz gave me money when he learned that I hadn't received a paycheck in several weeks while working for the Detroit Lions. He was the head coach of the Lions, and when he found out that I was not making any money because I had maxed out all my hours, he wrote me a check that day. If you are fortunate to have accumulated a life of wealth, hopefully, you have found ways to make your good fortune a blessing to others as well.

These are but a few lessons that have helped me understand the power and the value of being a humble leader. The humility habit will lead you to become not only a better leader but a better person. As we practice humility, we can see the benefits that it brings not only to us but to others. I could tell you about times when people have spoken to high schools or at local events where they know it's going to make the kids' day, and all it takes is a donation of our time. I could tell you about some of the great leaders I've been around in sports and business who know the names of every one of their staff members' children. They know their spouses' names. They call them by name when they see them. I could tell you about people in massive leadership roles who have come up to my children and humbly said, "I'm really fortunate to work with your dad." I could tell you what that means from a personal standpoint and how critical it is to surround yourself with people who apply the habit of humility.

Humility is a common separator for high achievers. It's a multiplier that allows us to achieve great things because it encourages others to want to follow us. That is the most critical factor for effective leadership: when others choose to follow you. Countless people, through humility, have been able to earn the right to be a leader. Sean McVay is an example of someone who does a phenomenal job and has always deflected praise during press conferences. I believe that a great leader will always deflect praise and embrace critique. You have to be humble enough to let the light shine on others. Praise them in public and critique them in private. This demonstrates a level of respect and care that will be appreciated by the people you lead.

A humble leader understands the importance of this and does not embarrass anyone. A great leader will always deflect praise, and they will also be humble enough to take coaching in front of the team. It takes an incredible leader, a person with true humility, to be able to be coached. I believe that no one is above being coached, regardless of your job title, stature, or net worth. If you think you are, I challenge you that you probably need coaching more than anyone. Finding ways to develop a learning habit is critically important for anyone interested in improving. I have sought out people and groups that offer this invaluable resource in a variety of ways. I have been fortunate to participate in numerous leadership groups that bring together people who are mutually interested in leaning into their growth mindset with others. Participating in such things allows me to become a better person and build a better version of myself, and this has helped me tremendously throughout my various leadership roles.

The Three People We Need in Our Lives

I regularly attend conferences, both virtually and in person. I also call colleagues and ask for advice. These are habits that help me tremendously. These are things that you can do to become a more productive individual. But the first step is humility. We must humbly accept that we are not where we need to be and that we can improve. I have discovered that we all need three people in our lives: a mentor, a mentee, and a healthy competitor. I say "healthy competitor" because we've all probably been in situations where competition has driven us, sometimes not in a healthy way. I challenge you to zoom out, as our previous chapter taught us, and allow yourself to see how a healthy competitor can develop in you the things that will help you improve. Let's take a closer look at these three important roles.

The Mentor

A mentor is someone you should be able to look to and learn from. This is typically someone who has achieved things that you are aiming to achieve or who sits in a seat that you desire to be in. You should have people in your life who are willing to mentor you and who are humble enough to give you the knowledge that they have gained. A more important part of this is the lessons they have learned because the mistakes that they have made will be learning material for you. As we avoid stumbling through obstacles, we can learn from mentors who have preceded us. This allows us to see the opportunities and decisions that we may have to make at some point in our journey to become a better version of ourselves.

The Mentee

At the same time, when you bring a mentee into your life, it forces you to learn at a much higher and faster rate. Digesting and then passing on information to those who are looking to learn from you requires a great understanding of the material. You must be on point. You have to attack that knowledge and understand it. It takes humility to step back and say, "I need to learn this a little bit better if I am going to give it to someone else."

It takes true humility to see things from both a mentor's and mentee's point of view. Once again, I urge you to use zoomability to see this: *How is my mentor leading me? How is my mentee learning from me?* This will allow you to humbly accept the areas that you may have to improve and the knowledge you need to learn a little bit better before you spread it to others.

The Healthy Competitor

Finally, there's the healthy competitor. Who do you have in your life with whom you can compete in a healthy manner? Who is challenging you and driving you to become a better version of yourself? What do they do? They don't always have to do the same thing as you. They could be colleagues. They could be a family member. They could be someone from high school whom you trust completely, or they might work in a completely different industry.

Whoever they are, the healthy competitor challenges you to sharpen your tools and gain that edge so that you can become a better version of yourself. They will drive you. They will support you in times when you need it—and we all have those times. Find someone in your life who's going to raise you up when you know that you have a little bit more to give. They will challenge you. They will drive you crazy at times, but they will also be there to help you pick up the pieces when you inevitably fall apart.

The beauty of humility in these three relationships is that it allows you to stay grounded. When others witness your humility, it will benefit them as well. When we humble ourselves and do good things, we feel good. When others benefit from our humility, they feel good. When we combine these things, we're going to spread good throughout the world, and we're going to become more humble because we see the benefit that it's having—not just on us but on everyone else. This helps create positive momentum for others to display humility.

The Humble Leader

Every strong culture I've ever been a part of has had leaders who demonstrate a great level of humility. Being a humble leader is one of the most important aspects of creating a successful, healthy culture that thrives on success and gains momentum. When you have the humility to admit that you have flaws as a leader, it allows everyone else to admit their mistakes.

Once you earn trust and allow yourself to show authentic vulnerability within your habits, you will drive humility to another level in your culture. It doesn't matter if you are the CEO or an entry-level employee. Once you show humility, it allows others to do the same. However, don't confuse humility with simply doing the right thing. Moving over to make room for someone on the bus is simply doing the right thing. However, when we choose to make a personal sacrifice for someone else's benefit when no one else will ever see or hear about it, this is true humility. No ulterior motives exist when there's true, authentic humility.

What are some practical ways that you can practice humility? Speak about yourself less. Don't join in gossip. Take the high road. Don't try to manage other people's lives. If they ask you for help, humbly listen. If they ask you for any advice, humbly give a small amount of advice and then listen some more. When you're listening, listen to understand; don't listen to respond. Have the humility to realize that you can learn from everyone you come into contact with. Get rid of the fear of missing out. Accept critical feedback with a smile. This is challenging, but you need to get over yourself. Say thank you when someone is willing to make you a better version of yourself. Give grace when others make a mistake. Give grace to yourself when you make a mistake. Accept and move on when something does not go your way. Do your best to find areas of improvement and then attack them relentlessly.

One story that I really love to tell is about Andrew Whitworth. "Whit" had a Hall of Fame-caliber career. Currently, he's on TV and doing some great things in life, but the one thing I want to point out about Whit is that he won the Walter Payton NFL Man of the Year Award. This is probably the single biggest award that you can get in the

NFL because it's about helping others. Obviously, the NFL provides players and coaches with an amazing platform. Andrew Whitworth has taken this platform and maximized it because he has found value in helping others and leaned into it.

We've already mentioned the incredible amount of adversity that our team encountered during the 2018 California wildfires and a local shooting that took place near our practice facility. Once we moved the game from Mexico back to Los Angeles, that Monday night football crowd would witness one of the greatest football games in regular season history. It was an unbelievable experience, one of my favorite games that I've ever been a part of. That includes the Super Bowls and some of the other bigger moments in my career. As mentioned earlier, Kevin Demoff and the leadership within the Los Angeles Rams organization, including owner Stan Kroenke, decided to give away the tickets to all first responders because of their dedication and the pain and suffering they had gone through, not only that week but through the entire wildfire season.

Without telling anyone, Andrew Whitworth took it upon himself to donate his entire game check to the families of those who had lost loved ones in the mass shooting. A guy like that doesn't want the spotlight. He doesn't do these things for the recognition. Instead, he does these things behind closed doors so that no one will ever see. When you put others first, you will be recognized whether you want to or not because, eventually, someone is going to tell your story. Andrew Whitworth is just that. I have the utmost respect for him and am absolutely honored to have worked with him.

When we talk about humility, we talk about getting outside of ourselves. It's one of the most difficult things that we experience in life because we are selfish by nature, and I'm including myself more than anyone else in this conversation. As we begin the struggle to become more selfless, we eventually get to the point where we say, "How do I do this?" Well, a simple question to ask is, "What's one thing that I did for someone today? Not for myself but for someone else?"

Simple Acts of Humility

What are some of the things that you can do that are simple? They really take no effort. Some take a small financial investment, and if you have the finances, I urge you to do it. Have you paid for someone's meal at a restaurant without them knowing? Few things are more satisfying than seeing the expression on their face when they realize it. Have you left a big tip for a waiter or a waitress who has fallen on hard times or who did an incredible job? Watching the joy that fills their face when they see what you've done is one of the most rewarding things I've experienced.

When you do have the opportunity to impact someone's day like that, to bring joy and excitement into their lives, it's your responsibility as a human to do that. If you don't have the financial resources, that's okay. Do you participate in volunteer work? Do you coach Little League teams? Do you find time to volunteer your time where able? Time is the most valuable resource we have because we are only given so much. What you do with that time matters a great deal.

Another thing you can do that costs very little is to give away blessing bags. This is something my wife taught me. She learned this technique through the wife's Bible study program when we were with the Miami Dolphins. The group put together blessing bags, which contained simple things like food, toiletries, and water. The bags were designed for those who had fallen on tough times, specifically the homeless. You'd keep them in your car and hand them out when you saw someone in need. Giving these bags away taught my whole family the importance of having compassion and empathy for our fellow humans. Staying humble can be difficult in the competitive world that we live in, but when you make it a habit to put others in front of yourself, it leads to long-term gratitude—not only does it put you in a better place, but it helps others, too.

The Importance of Gratitude

Humility at home is just as important. Whether you're married or single, whether you have kids or not, we all have relationships in our lives, and I challenge you to lean into them. I try to stay humble in my relationship with my wife, Robin. What's something that she's done that I've taken for granted? Well, I take for granted a lot of what she does for our children. One very important thing she does is, she gets them ready every day. I'm usually at work very early in the morning, so I miss a lot of those opportunities. And the amount of work that she has to put in just to get our kids out the door is amazing. So, what is one thing that I can appreciate her for and thank her for? Packing the kids' lunch. I know it sounds like a simple act, but that little act puts our children in a better place. So, I challenge you to find the things in your life that you may be taking for granted. Take a step back, zoom out, find someone you appreciate, and then tell them how thankful you are for them.

One way to help you do this is to add a gratitude journal to your daily practice. I've done this and have found great value in it. The challenge is not to repeat anything. Find something new every single day. List out at least one thing. If you feel up to it, list out three every day, whatever works for you. Just be sure to commit to this exercise every day. These could be simple, everyday items that you would otherwise overlook.

One of the things I wrote down recently was being grateful for our refrigerator. This came from a true point of gratitude because, shortly after I took a job with the Philadelphia Eagles and we moved into our home in New Jersey, a coastal storm came through and knocked out power for multiple days. When the power was finally restored, our refrigerator wasn't working properly. This was also in the midst of the COVID-19 pandemic. Working through homeowner's insurance and attempting to get parts sent and repairs scheduled took great effort. We went weeks without the use of our refrigerator, and I'm grateful to have it back.

We take countless things for granted each day, but when you take a step back and find a new perspective of gratitude, it can help you create a mindset of humility. This will allow you to find value, gratitude, and joy in some of the things that you might be taking for granted. One area that I have found to be very beneficial in helping me maintain an attitude of humility is doing random acts of kindness.

My challenge to you is simply to do one act of random kindness today. Normally, in books like this, you'll find a challenge for continued change. My ask is that today, the day you read or hear this, you perform a random act of kindness before you go to bed. If you're reading this at nighttime, you're screwed. Just joking. But get out of bed and pre-set breakfast for your family, or maybe set up the coffee machine for a spouse or a loved one. Handwrite a card or a note to a mentor. Send a generous text message or email to someone, or set a timer for doing something tomorrow morning. Whatever you do—DO IT!

My challenge is this: do not let your head hit the pillow, and don't let those eyes close before you do this task. The bottom line is that you must choose to humbly look past yourself at this very moment and simply act for someone else.

At the end of each day, you should look at yourself critically in the mirror and honestly assess your performance. Do this with true humility. It takes great humility to assess yourself critically, and it takes even greater humility to ask people you trust to critique your performance.

This could be a performance on a recent work-related project. This could be your performance in a board review. This could be your performance as a father, mother, husband, or wife. It takes great humility to bring others into your life who you trust to make you a better version of yourself. It also takes humility to listen when others criticize you. Remember that no one is above being coached. Humbly step back and say, "Okay, what can I learn from this situation, and how will I embrace it? Then, how can I put action to this so that I can truly become a better version of myself and improve for the people I care about?"

Call to Action
Humility

- Create a calendar reminder once a month with the following prompts.
  - What's one thing that I did this month that my younger self would make fun of me for? I believe it's important that we bring humor into these situations. Once we do, it allows us to move past our emotions, disengage, and think, *Okay, I see why this is absolutely ridiculous; I can't believe I did that.* Allow room to laugh at yourself.

  _____

  _____

  _____

  - Next, I want you to write down one thing that you did this month that your younger self would be proud of you for.

  _____

  _____

  _____

This will help you disengage, remain humble, and look at yourself with that same zoomability: "Okay, I've done some things that I need to improve, but I've also done some good things." Allow yourself to see both sides of this equation to become the best version of yourself. Once you make this a regular practice, you will gain momentum moving forward. As we apply humility to our daily habits, the next chapter will take us down the humble path of embracing discomfort.

CHAPTER 6

Getting Out of Your Comfort Zone

Leaning into stress is an art. Stress often gets a bad rap because everyone is afraid of it. People fear stress and adversity, but the fact of the matter is that no matter what we do, we will encounter it. What you do in such times is the most important thing. There's a great quote by American pastor and author Charles Swindoll: "Life is 10% what happens to you and 90% how you react to it." I challenge us all to take a step back, zoom out, and see stress and adversity as things that we can overcome but also that we can lean into and become better from. Don't just get through stress and adversity—pull what you can from them to become a better version of yourself.

The first step is to complete this challenge. Take out a pen or pencil, piece of paper, or digital iPad—whatever you use to take notes. I need you to write your first, middle, and last name. Once you have done that, I want you to switch hands. Put the pen, pencil, or stylus into your non-dominant hand and do the same thing. Write down your first, middle, and last name.

_____

_____

Once you do, in all likelihood, you'll laugh at yourself because your scribbles will resemble something like a first-grade child's handwriting or worse.

Enjoy the laughter for a moment. Then, look at that writing again and ponder this question: if you lost the ability to use your dominant hand today, how would you choose to go forward in life? Would you sulk and feel sorry for yourself? Would you step back and say, "Why me?" Would you think about all the things that you will not be able to do in life? It's natural to have those feelings and emotions, and it's important to honestly recognize them.

Now, keeping that pen or pencil in your non-dominant hand, I want you to write these words: "I choose to lean into stress."

_____

If you're like me, seeing the different handwriting styles will drive the point home: if you did lose your dominant hand, what would you do? I challenge you to keep this visual reminder. Put it away in your mental vault, where you can look at it and reflect on it when needed, and then find gratitude for what you have. Here's an addition to this challenge for overachievers: go through a whole day without using your dominant hand. Pretend that you have lost the ability. Gain the perspective of appreciation and gratitude, and then, when the next stressful moment of adversity arrives, lean into it with the confidence that you can overcome anything.

Doing the Hard Thing

I challenge everyone to do hard things often. One of my favorite non-fun things to do is expose myself to cold water, whether it's through immersion, plunging, or cold showers. This is also what part of my career has become. I've become known as the short-sleeved guy on NFL sidelines in certain instances, which is funny to me. People often ask me, "Why don't you wear long sleeves on the sideline, especially when coaching in a place like Philadelphia, where you play a lot of cold-weather games?" My answer to this question can be summed up by this quote by Bill Bowerman, a co-founder of Nike: "There's no such thing as bad weather, just soft people."

Now, that might sound meathead-ish or just plain stupid to a lot of people, and I'm certainly not recommending that you go out in below-sub-zero temperatures with exposed skin. Don't subject yourself to hypothermia. Don't try to sue me for getting sick or losing a finger to frostbite. But I do challenge you to do hard things.

I challenge myself in this way for two reasons. The first is that, in the back of my mind, I don't want to do it, and I despise the moments when my mind goes into fear or avoidance mode and tells me what I shouldn't do and what I can't do. That's usually when I lean into the discomfort with urgency. This mentality has helped me in many situations.

The second reason is that I'm building connections with our players. I remember a specific game when Zach Paschal, a wide receiver for us in Philadelphia during our NFC Championship season in 2022, was standing on the sideline in December at Chicago's Soldier Field. It was about three degrees Fahrenheit, well below freezing. Chicago is one of the coldest stadiums in the entire league, and when you hit the month of December, you should get your mind ready for an extremely chilly environment. And when there's a brisk wind, it's really not fun (the Windy City is a fitting nickname).

As usual, I was in short sleeves for this game. Zach was, too. In between series, when it's cold, players will often sit on the heated bench, stand by the heater on the sideline, or put on one of the massive jackets the team provides. So, Zach was wearing one of those jackets as we waited for a kickoff after a TV timeout. Sidenote: TV timeouts may be the most despised part of professional football games when it's freezing. He said to me, "You're freezing, aren't you?"

"ZP," I replied, "I'm so freaking cold! This is miserable!"

"Man, you're crazy," he said.

"Yeah," I told him, "but I'm gonna ride with you because I know you're cold, too."

As you can see, leaning into adversity not only creates that connection point but also builds resilience. Don't shy away from uncomfortable situations. I challenge you to lean into them. These things will make you stronger. Then, once you've completed that task, you'll be more apt and able to finish your next task.

I love challenging myself through very difficult workouts as well. How often do you just kick your own butt physically? How often do you go through extremely difficult physical tasks? How often do you want to quit, but refuse? When you refuse to quit, when you find a way to grow through adversity and pull from it everything that you need, you discover a more resilient version of yourself on the other side.

One of the things that led me to be able to be in short sleeves on a December day in Chicago when it's literally freezing is something that my high school friend and I called the "cold test." Growing up in southeastern Michigan, we were not shy of cold weather. We had to embrace it because it was there. When the winter hit, it was cold. One of the things my friend and I did that is definitely not recommended—and please don't do this!—is roll down the windows of my sweet 1990 Ford Escort in the middle of winter, usually around the coldest days, turn the air conditioning on full blast, and hang an arm out the window. Just as if it were a summer day at 80 degrees, we would sit back and relax while the freezing wind turned our arms into more purple versions of what they had looked like five minutes before.

Why would we do this? First, I will admit that youth, immaturity, and a level of not wanting to look like a wimp to your friend will lead you into some interesting situations. As we did this, I realized, *Man, we can get through some pretty tough stuff.* Once again, I'll add in my disclaimer: I am not recommending that you do this. I'm just giving you a little bit of insight into what's developed me into the adult version of myself that you see today.

One of the other things that I look back and reflect on fondly is doing heat runs in the summer. Not only did they help develop my mindset, but they also strengthened my physical body. I would wait until the hottest part of the day for my runs. This began in high school. It would be in the summer when we had optional workouts and were getting ready for football training camp to start sometime around the August reporting date. I would run for 30 minutes to an hour, which, once again, is not recommended when preparing for an anaerobic sport like football, but these are some of the details that you learn as you get into high-performance and elite-level training. I had no clue what I was doing in high school, but I do believe these simple tasks helped me sharpen my mind so that I could embrace adverse moments better later in life.

I was strengthening my body from an aerobic capacity standpoint, but more importantly, I was going through a very tough physical challenge to see how I would show up. Some of the things that I continue to do today are based on creating intentional discomfort. I love doing stadium stairs before every game—and sometimes hate it at the same time. Throughout my career, I have bounced back and forth between either running on the field or running in the steps of the seating sections when we get to the stadium early. When I run on the field, I typically run 20 x 100-yard sprints intermixed with at least two hundred push-ups in the end zones.

One thing that I really enjoy is walking into an NFL-sized stadium and seeing all the steps. It can be intimidating, just like a lot of things in life. But I take a one-step-at-a-time approach. I literally touch every step on the way up and then again on the way down. I don't snake through alternating sections; I make it a point to physically touch each step twice. I go up and down each flight of stairs just for my mentality, just to know that I've touched every step and I'm not skipping any. When my mind wanders, and I catch it, I say to myself, "One step at a time, one step at a time." Then I refocus, zoom out, zoom back in, and remember that if I take it one step at a time. Eventually, that set of stadium stairs will come to an end, and I'll be ready to attack the next challenge.

Turning Stress to Success

As you lean into some of these stressful environments, How can you turn that stress into success? Here's an example of when I was able to turn a stressful situation into a successful one. During my college recruiting process, I was in a very unique situation where I was considering playing for schools from Division I all the way down to Division III. At first, I was leaning toward a few Division II schools that were discussing potential partial scholarships because that would help my family immensely from a financial perspective. Eventually, though, I decided to attend a smaller Division III school because I could have an immediate impact on the team, and I loved the coaching staff.

As we went through the process, I began summer workouts with the team, started getting to know some of my teammates, and took care of scheduling everything, like dormitory roommates and other logistics. The financial aspect was one thing, but then we also got into the academic piece. There was a major shift, so my anticipated major, which was physical therapy at the time, was not going to be offered at the school in the upcoming semester. So, I said, "What's next? What do I do?" The answer?—I made a shift and chose to adapt. This was an uncomfortable shift because, at that point, I had become friends with a lot of my teammates. Eventually, I decided on the University of Toledo, where I chose to walk on to the football team. Ultimately, I enjoyed my time there and had an amazing experience. Going there had a huge impact on my life, helping me in several ways get to where I am today.

One person I met there was Steve Murray, the head strength and conditioning coach at the time. He helped me get an opportunity with the Detroit Lions, which got me into the NFL and ultimately led me to the multiple stops that I've had around the league. This brought me to the journey that I've been afforded throughout my career. This has been awesome to reflect upon because, although it was difficult, especially for an 18-year-old kid, making tough decisions with an urgent mentality and then attacking the situation relentlessly and making the best of it has allowed me to get to where I am today and where I am going from here. A default attitude of urgency and attacking opportunities are things that we all have to carry with us. How can we turn stress into success? By leaning into it. We are afforded the opportunity to thrive under tension when we do this, and we can grow through adversity. That is adaptation. Just as diamonds are formed through pressure, we can transition into a stronger version of ourselves through the application of stress and tension.

When we don't shy away from stress but embrace it and dive in, control what we can, and lean into it, we will find adaptation. Adaptation occurs in our lives just like it does with a diamond. It transforms us into better and more capable versions of ourselves so that we can handle the next bout of stress or adversity that's around the corner.

Lean into Stress and Adversity

I've had a few significant periods of adversity in my life. One occurred in 2018. It was an early spring day in May, and we were in the middle of our off-season training with the Rams. We were building what would become a Super Bowl team, and life was great. I had come off some individual awards and accolades. Our team was doing extremely well. We had overachieved significantly from what the outside world, the media, and everyone else had anticipated that we would be able to do in that first season in Los Angeles. As I went through this day, everything was normal. I woke up at a very early hour, got my workout in, and prepared myself mentally and physically for the day.

I vividly remember sitting in our team meeting, which we started the day with. This was a Monday. As I watched Sean's presentation, my vision was blurry, and I started to feel nauseous. I leaned over to our medical director, Reggie Scott, and said, "Reggie, something's not right."

He grabbed me and took me out of the room. In the hallway, I began to vomit. Something was off. We walked to the training room, and when we reached the medical examination area, Reggie said, "It's probably viral. You know, this happens sometimes."

"It's never happened to me," I replied, "but okay."

He recommended that I lie down, so I did for a few moments. Eventually, I got back up, but I immediately became nauseous again. I went to Reggie and said, "Something's not right." At that point, we called the team doctor, who, out of an abundance of precaution, said that someone should take me to the hospital to get checked out. The hospital was about an eight- to ten-minute drive from our facility, depending on traffic. By the time we got there and they wheeled me into the emergency room, I'd lost the ability to speak—I was having a stroke!

I was in my early 30s and dominating life. I had the role of a lifetime and my dream job. My family and I were living in Los Angeles, California. Our third child had just turned one. I had a young family and a beautiful wife at home. I had all these things going for me, but I was sitting in a hospital room with around 15 medical personnel rushing around me. When you look up and there are 15 people in an emergency room, you begin to think, *This is probably not good.*

Bits and pieces of what I went through are still unclear—my memory's fuzzy—but what I do remember vividly is at one point sitting in the intensive care unit and watching a priest walk down the hallway. I still don't know to this day if he was going to administer "last rites" to someone else in the ICU. I don't know what the story was with the other patients there. I don't know a lot, but what I do know is that the picture I painted in my mind that day will never leave my memory.

As I sat there and reflected upon my situation, it helped me to repaint the picture of what's important. I was able to zoom in and zoom out at that moment, and I thought, *Wow, what am I going to do moving forward? I have a second chance.* The doctors injected a clot buster that prevented long-term damage, and thank God, there was none. I stayed in the ICU for a few days and was out and back to work the next week. This was a tough time because I felt invincible at that age, and a lot was going on professionally and personally. This was an opportunity to refocus and lean into that stress. They found that I had a hole in my heart. The following year, I had a procedure to have it closed. I never thought I would be having heart surgery in my 30s.

This was a situation that I was able to learn from. It allowed me to realize, hey, medical situations don't always discriminate based on whatever your age is, whatever your personal health risk is. Sometimes, tough things happen. Being prepared to lean into stress and adversity when they do strike allows you to jump in. So, how do we let the situation make us stronger? I know there were things that I could actually reflect upon and write about. How would this make me a stronger individual? It would give me a better appreciation for life. It would help me be more empathetic to teammates, players, coaches, fellow workers, and employees. It would allow me to see things from a zoomed-out perspective so I could apply better empathy and gratitude to my day-to-day life.

How would this make me a better person? There are a lot of ways to lean into that stress. The top five stressors in life are the loss of a loved one, divorce, moving, a major illness or injury, and job loss. Many of us have dealt with at least one of these. All these things occur on a day-to-day basis, and a lot of people are currently struggling with them right now. Growth occurs through stress. Whether we choose to face these situations or not, it is up to us how we lean into them and respond. Adaptation is necessary if we want to move forward. Attacking adaptation with a growth mindset will allow us to take from the situation the things that can help us improve. One of the ways that we can do this is by consistently presenting mini-adversity into our lives. As I mentioned, I like to do this through workouts. I also love attending conferences and clinics with like-minded people.

Connecting through Stress

I enjoy thoroughly surrounding myself with people with a growth mindset. One of the things that I have found immense pleasure in is going through group workouts with these people at events. One of these happened recently. It was at an event with a friend of mine named Ryan Hawk who is an author and host of a great podcast, *The Learning Leader Show*. Ryan puts on a yearly event for several like-minded individuals. At this particular one, we had a number of people attend a yoga sculpt class in a hot yoga room in Columbus, Ohio. This was a challenging workout, and I remember sweating profusely next to all the other fellow attendees. As we continued to put forth effort in that uncomfortable environment, we found humor, we found joy, and we found appreciation in the fact that we were all struggling in our own ways. Find the strength to get through situations in moments of discomfort. It's when you want to quit that you need to lean into it. If you do, you will pull something from it both at that moment and later in life.

Another good friend of mine, Ben Newman, goes through a grueling daily workout that he has defined as the "unrequired workout." This workout is INTENSE! I have been through it multiple times. It takes approximately an hour to complete and consists of several exercises that will have even the most fit individual questioning their ability to finish, including a plank hold for almost five minutes straight. I have immense respect for Ben because, as of this writing, he has done it for almost 1,800 consecutive days. This workout is definitely uncomfortable. I don't recommend it for the faint of heart or those not practicing a regular exercise routine. But, if you're willing, it is a great opportunity to win that self-negotiation that will certainly come during this workout.

Another one of the great mini-adversity moments that I've experienced happened again in 2018. It was on that same trip to Colorado Springs as we were preparing for the Mexico City game, which I mentioned in earlier chapters. In Colorado Springs, there is a steep uphill hike simply known as "the Incline." It is actually the Manitou Incline just outside the city. It's a hike. Wooden railroad ties are nailed into the mountain for about a mile. You gain approximately two thousand feet of elevation, and at the summit, you are roughly 8,500 feet above sea level. Then, there is a four-mile trail back down once you reach the peak. The record for getting to the very top is 17 minutes. Most of the Olympians who train in nearby Colorado Springs at the United States Olympic Committee complete this in the low 30s. The first time I ever attempted it was on this trip, and I did it with a group of people. It took me 36 minutes, and I was MAD because I'm a little psychotic and felt like I should be up there with the Olympians. I'm not saying that I'm realistic; I'm just psychotic. Once again, we all have an ego (haha).

As we climbed up the mountain path, my heart rate was averaging between 160 and 170 for the entire 30+ minutes, and I thought, *I can slow down, take it easy, and step off the gas, or I can keep pushing*. Then I reflected and found the why, and I started mentally repeating to myself: *Lean into this stress. This is going to make me better. This is going to make me a better version of myself.*

Just after the wildfires and mass shooting occurred, my family and I were getting our family Christmas pictures taken, an annual tradition for us. When we lived in California, we did this at our local mall.

As my wife and I waited patiently with our three children to have our photos taken, we noticed a young person walk up to the desk. Because we were right next to the counter, we overheard the person explain that they had recently taken their family pictures. However, one of the family members had passed away in the recent mass shooting. They had been there weeks earlier, taking pictures with a full family. Now they were picking up those family photos and returning to a home where the family was no longer intact.

If you want a new perspective, you need to zoom out, look at what other people are going through, and find value in the stress and adversity that comes up in your life. These things can make us stronger; they can make us tougher. Once again, I'm not saying that we would choose to go through many of these things, but is there an attitude that we can adopt that will allow us to take the adversity and use it to become better versions of ourselves? Absolutely.

Developing Resiliency

Methods to increase our resiliency are all around us. They are abundant. Do you take cold showers? Do you do daily workouts, especially on the days when you don't want to? What about that early morning wake-up, the toe test? Do you hit snooze? Challenge yourself. Find those daily wins. It's stressful at the moment, but lean into that stress. Don't hit snooze. Get up and go. Do you practice sound nutritional habits? Make the right decision. Turn away from the dessert. Don't lean into negative or unhealthy habits, but really lean into positive ones. Look at your social media habits and honestly reflect on them. Are you leaning into the easy scrolls? Are you tapping on stuff that you shouldn't? Continue to challenge yourself. Do you spend unnecessary time on mindless posts?

When adversity strikes, it can be in large or small doses. It could be a great amount of adversity and a life-altering change, or it could be a very small one like hitting snooze on your alarm clock. Whatever it is, we have the opportunity to answer. Remember what Charles Swindoll said: our attitude is 90% of the situation. Only 10% of life is what happens to us. We all have a choice. Will we feel sorry for ourselves in those moments? Will we sleep in? Will we fall into unhealthy habits? Will we expect everyone to feel sorry for us? The sad truth is that a lot of people will feel sorry for us. I challenge you to put better friends in your life. Surround yourself with people who are going to be there but are also going to help you. If you want warm milk and a warm snuggle, get a dog. Just joking. As a side note, I have a dog, and he's sitting right next to me. Warm milk, not so much. I don't usually drink that.

The other opportunity comes in the form of a simple choice. Choose to attack adversity head-on with an urgent attitude. Default to urgency in everything that you do, especially in the midst of adversity and stress. This will lead to immense personal growth and develop grit. Don't just lean in—jump in.

When we make it a mission to form daily habits through aggressive and persistent repetition, we will become better. It has to be aggressive because this is how you break through bad cycles of habits. Bad habits develop through persistent patterns over time. Consistency, however, is the key to breaking these poor habits. Consistency is one of the best measurements of all performance. You can apply this to almost any endeavor. Consistently saving money has built a fortune for people like Warren Buffett. Consistently applying aggressive work habits has allowed people like Kobe Bryant to maximize their talents and win multiple championships. Consistent messaging and aggressively hitting the campaign trail have allowed people to become political leaders who have changed the world. How can you apply consistency to improve your life?

Your Call to Action.

- *Option One:* Create a 20-minute routine that you will follow and commit to for the next 50 days.
  - This can include reading, writing, meditating, taking a gratitude walk outside, hot-cold contrast baths, etc. The choices are nearly endless, but the most important step is to take ACTION.
  - No days off, no negotiation, no excuses. You will complete this task for 50 days in a row. Commit to YOURSELF!
- *Option Two:* Whatever your current exercise commitment is, challenge yourself to add ten minutes of activity every single day for the next 50 days. If your current routine is zero, then exercise for ten minutes a day. If you currently exercise for an hour and a half every day, bump it up to an hour and 40 minutes.

For option two, I recommend some form of static exercise. These exercises are great for physical and mental training. For example, combine a wall sit with various planking positions. When you put yourself in a physically demanding position, self-negotiation begins. Your mind will want to negotiate an easier path. But it is YOUR CHOICE! When you find yourself in that situation, get out of your comfort zone and shut down the negotiation before it begins. With a default urgent mentality, just do the work!

As we look forward to the next chapter, we will learn the impact that self-discipline can have on our lives. We will also learn how to apply daily deposits to our routine, which will lead to continued growth.

CHAPTER 7

The Habit of Discipline: Daily Deposits

How do we win our days? We do it through daily deposits. Our daily actions will lead to long-term habits. This is what we have to deposit every day. We don't rise to goals; instead, we fall to our systems. This is how we avoid letting one bad day turn into multiple.

Analyze your current system. What's your positive-growth checklist?

Spiritual, mental, and physical. Number one, spiritual: Did you pray or meditate today? Physical: Did you work out for at least 30 minutes today? Mentally: Did you stimulate your mind and interests through growth practices? This could be things like reading, writing, playing a musical instrument, or listening to a podcast—anything that stimulates your mind and thought processes.

The Three Ws

We start with the three Ws: **worship, working out, and writing.** The three Ws offer a framework for building better habits throughout your life, and mastery of them leads us to the fourth W: WINNING. So, it's critical to choose habits that align with the successes that we are aiming for. We are what we repeatedly do, so to become a better version of ourselves, we must attach healthy habits to our daily processes. All the best performers that I've ever been around have this in common: they are elite because their routines and daily habits are elite. They put in those daily deposits. Their habits are simple but not easy. It takes aggressive patience to stick with good habits over a long period.

Worship

I'm a Christian. Regardless of your religious practices, taking time to reflect spiritually each day is a practice that we should all participate in. Taking time each day to praise God and read His Word allows me to focus my energies so that I am in a mindset to help others. Starting our days with a positive reflection about something bigger than ourselves lets humility and gratitude flow throughout our work. This is the first W on the list because it is the most important.

Workout

We should all be in the practice of doing difficult things. This helps to sharpen our minds and bodies. Building a daily routine that includes intentional time to work out will help us develop grit throughout our lives. From a physiological perspective, there are countless health benefits to doing this, but the benefits extend far beyond becoming a healthier person. There will inevitably be times and days when your motivation is lacking. This is an opportunity to overcome the reasons and the excuses that others often use to convince themselves that skipping a workout is okay.

While we need to always be prepared to give ourselves grace in moments of failure, making the right choice daily and sticking to your routine of hard physical work will lead you to become a more consistent performer in life. The mental benefits of working out are also significant, from the endorphin release to the confidence we develop through a positive fitness habit. Getting healthy and working out is one of the most vitally important aspects that we can add to our daily habits. This daily deposit will lead to long-term growth and abundance.

Writing

I credit my friend Ryan Hawk, who I mentioned earlier, for inspiring me to take on this daily process. Ryan is an author and a podcast host who has done amazing things, and he speaks often about the benefits of creating a daily writing habit. The mental process that takes place when you routinely practice writing down your thoughts will challenge and engage you in new ways. Building a consistent writing practice into your schedule must be done intentionally.

Giving yourself writing prompts can help you develop this habit. My wife, Robin, has even come up with creative and thought-provoking prompts for me. Getting prompts from others will give you a chance to think outside your perspectives and open up more flexible thinking. This leads to you becoming more engaged as you navigate topics and questions that give your mind a mental gymnastics session.

There are many other ways to select unique writing prompts. One fun method is to select a random group of words and then write down thoughts revolving around them. You can even have family members or friends select the words for you. This can be quite entertaining if you get your children involved. Once you have selected the group of words, begin writing your thoughts. You can build stories around each word to interweave them. Give yourself the goal of writing a specific number of words each day, and then attack this habit to make it long-term. Discipline doesn't always have to be complicated.

Keep It Simple

How can you consistently apply positive deposits at work? By making them simple. When I was working for free for the Detroit Lions, I thought that getting a job in the NFL was a huge deal. I soon realized that not getting a paycheck for six months was also a big deal because those negative thoughts began to enter my mind. So, what did I reflect upon? The only thing that I could control was my attitude and effort. I wrote earlier about what my daily schedule entailed at that point in my career. Even though I wasn't getting paid, how I showed up was MY CHOICE! Part of my daily process was to try to be one of the first ones at work in Allen Park every single day. When I came in at approximately 4.30 a.m. on most days and flicked on the lights, I had the inner pride of being the first one there, ready to attack my duties and stack another day of positive daily deposits. I knew I was in the right place. It didn't matter if I was making a million dollars or zero dollars; I knew that all I had to control was my effort and attitude, which would eventually lead me to long-term success.

The daily discipline of being the first one in is one thing, but having a great attitude would lead me to better outcomes as well. What I did not do was complain about not getting a paycheck. I didn't do less work, and I definitely didn't take the easy way out and give up. When you attack every day with a consistent and relentless attitude, you will achieve the outcomes you desire. Discipline is about assessing and editing. How do you edit your life?

Lessons from Kobe

One of my favorite stories to tell about Kobe Bryant is from a time when he was speaking to the Alabama football team. I was blessed to be able to go out to the University of Alabama and consult with their football program on all their performance initiatives. I did this shortly after Kobe Bryant, unfortunately, passed away. They told me, "Kobe was just here recently, and he gave a presentation to our team. Would you like to see the video?"

"Absolutely!" I replied. So, with the entire team gathered in the auditorium, I got to sit in the back of the room and watch this video of a legend explaining his mental approach to becoming one of the best in his sport. Kobe talked about editing your life and went into the stories that summarized why he had formed this mental approach. You could see the passion in his eyes as he lit up with true reflection on how he edited his life every day. He talked about a couple of things that are extremely important for all of us to consider.

First, you must find the right people in your life. Do you have people in your life who are holding you back? You need to edit them out immediately. Do you have people in your life who are pushing you? Lean into them. Continue to lean into those relationships that you know will lead to long-term growth. Do you have activities and habits that are holding you back? What negative habits do you need to edit out of your life? What positive edits do you need to make? What positive habits do you need to add to your life? Once you identify these habits, pursue them relentlessly.

As Kobe talked, the players in the video sat in respectful silence, soaking in every word. Some players eventually raised their hands and posed great questions. One asked, "How did you attack your process when you were going up against certain opponents?" Kobe dove into a story about Allen Iverson and how a reporter once asked him, "Are you afraid of Allen Iverson dropping 30-plus points on you?" Kobe took great offense to that. "Afraid?" he said. "I'm not afraid of anyone."

After the interview, he asked himself, *What do I need to edit?* Later that night, he was watching television, and it was Shark Week on the Discovery Channel. I love Shark Week, so this sparked my curiosity. In the documentary he was watching, a great white shark attacked its prey from beneath the surface of the water. He said to himself, "That's what I need to edit. I need to edit my attack on defense." The next time that Kobe played Allen Iverson, he ended up attacking him just like that great white did, relentlessly pursuing him on defense. Ultimately, he got the outcome he desired, telling the players, "I don't think AI scored a point that game."

Persistence vs. Perseverance

As we continue to think about developing our perseverance through grit and determination, what kind of consecutive streaks can we put into practice within our daily lives? One person who I truly admire is Mike Birch, the COO of Speedway Motorsports. Mike has a consecutive days running streak of over nine years. He has literally not missed a day of running for nine years! That's incredible. I've mentioned Ben Newman and his consecutive workout streak of almost 1,800 days as of the writing of this book.

Persistence and perseverance are both important. Persistence is the short-term version of long-term perseverance. You can be persistent in a short-term task, such as a workout, work project, or homework assignment, but can you demonstrate perseverance through that process day after day, year after year? These friends are examples of perseverance. What habits do you have in your life right now where you may be persistent, but you're just off a little bit? You're missing maybe that fifth and sixth day; you're taking the weekends off. What habits can you stack and build into that perseverance practice? Perseverance is what will lead to the long-term outcomes you desire. As we develop our systems, the first areas of life where you can stack habits are exercise, nutrition, reading, writing, and beginning a gratitude journal.

These are simple areas in which we can begin to build a perseverance practice. Challenge yourself, stack habits, build in daily deposits that revolve around these areas, and build your mind, body, and soul through those three Ws. Exhibiting daily persistence through repeated actions will lead us to long-term perseverance, but we have to start now. This will also lead to bulletproof belief and confidence.

Earned confidence allows us to deflect negative opinions. We carry our confidence like a shield that deflects the arrows of negativity, doubt, and naysayers. Carry this shield proudly, but don't allow it to cover the sword of humility, which we should always carry with us. When we develop and combine this confident humility, we can freely dive into the areas that we know are not only best for us but also for those whom we are responsible for. Whether it's our teammates, employees, or family members, once we act with the intention of serving others through our disciplines, we give them the opportunity to achieve unbelievable things.

The Habit of Discipline

When thinking about the habit of discipline, Tom Brady comes to mind. What he was able to accomplish on the football field is simply amazing. It is hard to imagine anyone matching his achievements. I have never had the opportunity to work directly with Tom; in fact, he has beaten my teams on multiple occasions, including the Super Bowl. I have always been fascinated with high achievers and love to ask questions of those who have played with and coached players like Tom.

One of my favorite stories is about Tom's transition to the Tampa Bay Buccaneers. The year he guided them to an amazing playoff run and World Championship truly set Tom apart as a leader. Many of those who shared the locker room with him would go on to tell stories of daily text messages that they received from him. These texts typically revolved around mindset and establishing personal standards that would allow them to become the best players they could be.

When you consider the immense weight that a player of Tom's caliber already carries in their professional and personal life, learning that he took the time to send his teammates personal messages gives you an understanding of what small disciplines can do for an entire organization. By investing daily in his teammates, he built a fortune of confidence and belief in himself and the team. As the season unfolded and transitioned into the postseason, you could feel that belief come through in the style of play that his team exhibited.

Regardless of the sport that we are talking about, new players with tremendous talent come into the mix every single season. However, when you combine skill and passion in an individual who places worth on daily deposits, you get a once-in-a-generation leader. It has been fun to watch Tom compete (except when he was beating me in the playoffs multiple times), especially as a leader. I have the utmost respect for people like this who put the effort in, which they know will lead to a competitive advantage.

We can learn a lot from these lessons. As we attempt to establish a habit of discipline through our daily deposits, we can gain a humble confidence to carry with us. This will shield us from those who may try to tear us down or have negative things to say. Use that confidence, build it through your daily perseverance practice, and stack your habits so you know you can be relentless, not only in carrying that shield of confidence but also in your next step forward. Our daily habits must be in alignment with our long-term vision. The habits that we instill now will lead to the future outcomes that we receive.

When we focus on our daily process over the long term, we build the perseverance that will lead us to the outcomes that we desire. Being relentless with your personal standards will lead you to more daily deposits and more consistent habits that build success.

Call to Action # 1
End-of-Day Apology or End-of-Day Thank-You Note

- As you reflect at the end of a day and look at yourself critically in the mirror, ask yourself, *Is there someone who I need to apologize to?* If the answer is yes, apologize to that person with urgency and authenticity. If it's bedtime, send them a text; if you have to send them an email, find a way to follow through and take the important step of action.
- If you can't think of anything you need to apologize for, congratulations! Instead, who do you need to say thank you to? Who is one person in your life who has had a positive impact on you? Once you identify someone, send them a kind and thoughtful message explaining how they have helped you. This is one of the most impactful disciplines that you can add to your life.

Once you begin this practice, you will be amazed at how much it helps you gain better clarity and appreciation for others in your life—and how great the positive impact this simple act has on others. I hope that you, too, receive a few of these authentic and thoughtful notes at some point. When you do, you will gain a new appreciation for how much they mean.

Call to Action #2
Growth Moments

- What was a positive-growth moment from today? Look at yourself again in the mirror and ask. "What did I do well today? What can I pat myself on the back for? And what am I going to continue to add to my daily habits that will lead to long-term perseverance and ultimately give me the outcomes that I desire?"

  _____

  _____

- What was a negative-growth moment from today? Look at yourself critically and honestly. What was a moment that you need to edit for tomorrow?

  _____

  _____

Just like Kobe did, edit your life and do it now. Apply the urgency needed to make changes that will help you tomorrow, next week, next month, and years into your future. Applying this habit of discipline is what makes achieving your goals possible.

In the next chapter, we will learn from some of the great lessons of leadership that demonstrate how unique tools can help you drive positive outcomes.

CHAPTER 8

Leadership Lessons Learned

As I reflect on my life's journey so far, I always look back on my experiences through a specific lens. Once again, zoomability comes into play. I try to zoom out and zoom back in. I try to live my life as if I'm walking through a museum instead of rushing through an airport. When you take this approach, you allow yourself to appreciate the things around you. How many of us just go through life sprinting to the airport gate, trying to make sure that we're there for the plane to take off on time? Well, the beauty is that the plane's going to take off whether we're there or not. So, do we want to be on time? Absolutely. However, there is typically more than one flight option wherever we are going in life.

When we view life as spending time in a museum, it allows us to disconnect and zoom out from the rushed anxiety that fills our daily lives. We don't have to spend time with every painting or every work of art, but our willingness to be in the moment, to be where our feet are, and to appreciate our surroundings allows us to experience true gratitude. So, I challenge you to reflect: are you sprinting through an airport, trying to get to the next gate? Or are you taking your time? Are you embracing the attitude, still with urgency, that you are spending time in a museum where you can appreciate the things around you?

Lessons from Sean McVay

As we reflect on the previous chapters, we can zoom out and refocus our views. I can zoom out and see so many people who have had a profound influence on my perspectives in life and some of the leadership lessons that I've learned from others. Sean McVay, who's mentioned in this book, has done a phenomenal job as a leader. He's incredibly focused and commands respect within the NFL. When I think of Sean, I think of standards and humility. I think of how he sets his standards, going back to our early years with the Los Angeles Rams. The standard is the standard. The standard is what we allow through our daily habits and actions, and it's what we demonstrate to the people around us.

His first team meeting set the stage by establishing an incredibly high standard. He knows that with consistent daily habits and deposits, he will be able to maintain that perspective and those standards throughout the rest of his career. This includes calling out every player by name during team meetings, especially on Saturday nights before games, going into individual details about each player's game plan, and telling them how they're going to impact the game. He spends the time and energy to be fully prepared, setting the stage without ever needing to read off note cards, investing in the daily practices necessary to be ready in that moment.

Those are some of the small standards that Sean lives by every day. And that's why he has become one of the best head coaches in the recent history of the NFL. He is also incredibly humble. When we talk about the humility habit, he displays it every day through his actions. He allows staff members to present to the team. I remember vividly how, one year, he allowed several staff members, including me, to present to the team our core values. This ended with me presenting on competitive greatness, which was the tip of the pyramid that we used as our visual. Having the opportunity and the humility to sit there and step back and say, "I want these players to hear from everyone on our staff," truly shows how humble he is. He's built a culture based on "we," not me.

Sean also always says that the star of the team is the team. These are things that he believes, these are things that he lives by, and these are things that he demonstrates on a day-by-day basis. He praises others in press conferences, once again demonstrating his humility. He knows everyone's kids' and spouses' names, and he tells the kids how lucky he is to work with their fathers. He also tells players and staff members that he loves them—and he means it.

These are things that men in the NFL are not supposed to do, but Sean broke the mold, becoming truly who he is, setting standards, and having the humility to live by how he was raised. He welcomes other people, even staff members, into his home, allowing them to live with him for several months. These are some of the incredible stories that Sean has built into his daily process and habits, and this is part of the reason that he has become such an extremely successful head coach and leader.

Jim Schwartz

Another great example of a true leader is Jim Schwartz. I was fortunate to have him as my first head coach in the NFL when I worked with the Detroit Lions. I was young and in the early stages of developing my leadership perspectives; some of the things that I believe from a core value perspective, like zoomability, I learned from Jim Schwartz.

My first year with Coach Schwartz was in 2009. The previous year, the Lions had become the first team in NFL history to go 0 and 16. When we inherited this team, expectations were low. After we won two games that first year, sadly, some people celebrated the improvement, but it wasn't good enough for us. As Coach Schwartz zoomed out towards the tail end of that next 2010 season, we were sitting at two wins again—two and 10. We had four games left to play.

As we walked into our first team meeting that week, Coach Schwartz stood in front of the team and said, "Men, listen to me when I tell you that at this time next year, we will be playing meaningful football games in the city of Detroit in December and January." He was implying that we were going to be in the playoffs the following season. Something that had not happened for the Lions in well over a decade. He said, "I challenge you to look at these last four games as if we're in that situation right now. We need to build that rhythm, that callous, that grit, and that determination right now."

When he said this, every person in that room sat up in their chair, and I saw the belief begin to grow. I saw the confidence develop. In the first week, we got a great, gritty win. The second week, we stacked another one. The third week, another. Finally, the fourth week arrived, and we capped it off with our fourth victory in a row. We finished season six and 10. That doesn't sound impressive by NFL standards. However, the grit and determination that we built carried over to the following season.

We had a lockout during the off-season due to an ongoing negotiation over a new collective bargaining agreement. Coaches were not allowed to have any contact with the players. So, we missed a significant amount of time where we could have made the culture and grit of this team even stronger. However, once we returned, we didn't lose a game in the preseason. We didn't lose any of our first five competitions. In the sixth game, we lost a hard-fought and tough football game against the San Francisco 49ers, led by head coach Jim Harbaugh. After the game, there was the Harbaugh-Schwartz handshake, which is another story in and of itself.

Later that season, in December, we clinched a playoff berth at Ford Field in the city of Detroit. I still remember Jim Schwartz demonstrating the humility of being a leader of an NFL organization and telling our entire football team, "No one goes in the locker room. You stay out here on the field," as we clinched in front of our home crowd in a game against the San Diego Chargers. The entire team walked around the stadium and high-fived all the fans who had remained.

This was a moment of humility and a moment of thankfulness because Coach Schwartz understood the gratitude that we owed those fans. He also understood the magnitude of the moment. We had gone through so much adversity in the previous two seasons. We had found a way to win. We had found a way to believe. We had found a way to develop grit through our daily deposits, our daily habits, and the repetition of our actions. He zoomed out and he saw a full year in advance, and he made the entire team believe. I'll never forget that team meeting.

Other Leaders in My Life

Jim Caldwell is an amazing leader. He has been a head coach for multiple NFL and college football teams. I was fortunate to work for Coach Caldwell when he became the head coach of the Detroit Lions in 2014. When I reflect on his leadership, I think about discipline, daily deposits, and consistency. He's one of the most consistent coaches I've ever been around—in his reading, his exercises, his personal process, and how he attacks every day. He commands respect.

He had the humility to take out every position group to dinner during his first years as head coach. He gave several talks where he made us realize how appreciative we should be to have a role in the NFL, regardless of position, whether you're the highest-paid player on the team or the newest staff member. He displayed everything that it took to be consistent and build good daily deposits.

During my time with the Miami Dolphins I was able to learn from head coach Adam Gase. In 2016, he taught me a very valuable lesson about belief and leaning into those stressful and adversity-filled times. We started the season one and four in Miami. Eventually, though, we made the playoffs that year, which was extremely uncommon. Statistically, it is tough to make the playoffs when you start in that big of a hole. What Coach Gase did was lean into that adversity. He made tough decisions, and he did it with a default attitude of urgency. He made significant decisions based on player personnel. He cut players who were very talented but were not good for our culture at that time. His ability to believe in the moment and lean into the stress was incredible, and it helped allow the team to turn our season around.

I'll never forget the amazing lessons I learned from being on the head coach hiring committee for the Philadelphia Eagles in 2021. We interviewed several incredible candidates who went on to become head coaches around the league. We eventually hired Nick Sirianni who would lead our team to the Super Bowl in his second season. We all flew to South Florida on Mr. Lurie's jet to his home and interviewed candidates for about two weeks. Finally, Nick Sirianni's name popped up, and we called him. Typically, when you're interviewing a head football coach for an NFL organization, you send a private jet to pick them up. You wine and dine them, bring them in, and make a big deal of it. Nick happened to be vacationing in nearby Fort Lauderdale, Florida, when we reached out. He said, "No, I'm good. I don't need a car service or anything. I'll just drive up to you guys."

The next day, he drove up in a rented minivan because he has young children. He had stopped at a nearby department store and bought a shirt that definitely did not fit him well. In the interview, we noticed his authenticity. His core values were seared into his mind. He had scribbled notes down the night before, whereas most of these other candidates had had several days to prepare, and some of them had even brought binders and presentation materials. Nick, on the other hand, spoke from his heart. He told great stories, and we saw his talent for storytelling, his passion, his accountability beliefs, and how he was going to train the team and lead them to success. As we continued to talk with him on a second interview, we ultimately decided that he would be the man for the job.

I've learned so many things from other people—like Tom Lewand, who was the president of the Detroit Lions at the time. I was just getting started in my career, barely making any money, and had just proposed to my now wife, Robin; he allowed us to have the wedding reception at Ford Field at a significant discount. We are still grateful for that to this day and our wedding day was amazing. I still remember his daily routine. He would beat all the players into the facility and get in a workout every single day. He was one of the first people to arrive, sometimes around four in the morning. He would actually come into the weight room and do the players' workout for that day. The commitment, the daily deposits, and the daily habits he invested in were consistent with being successful.

Mike Tannenbaum, who is currently an analyst for ESPN, spent most of his career in high-level front-office positions, including general manager and executive vice president. I worked with Mike while we were in Miami. He reminds me of the importance of paying attention to others, sometimes having empathy, but also just reaching out and saying thank you. Mike had a great habit of sending a very personalized text message to each member of the Miami Dolphins staff on their birthday. In it, he would tell you what you meant to the organization and why he was thankful that you were there. He also set up family events in conjunction with head coach Adam Gase, like family bowling, family Christmas and holiday parties, and the Dolphins Day event that we would attend in the spring. Some of the things that they did with the support of Steven Ross, the owner, were incredible. It was one of the best family atmospheres I've been in.

Les Snead, general manager for the Rams, has a true growth mindset. I love how Les would bring in various authors to our training camp each year. We would schedule visits with people like Ryan Holiday, Jim Collins, Sam Walker, and Jon Gordon, people who would come in and teach us better habits. Les also believed in trusting his staff. He would allow everyone to do their job and never micromanage. He is thoughtful and intentional with his words. He truly cared about the details of interacting with everyone else, and his humility was always present.

I think about Stan Kroenke, the owner of the LA Rams, and the vision that he had for the new LA stadium, along with the many city developments that he has built and is continuing to build. I think about how he has done so many things for that city. I think about him chartering and spending an exorbitant amount of money just to get our families out of California during the wildfire season to join us in Colorado so that everyone had peace of mind and was safe. He's humble and acts behind the scenes.

I also think about the time when we were trying to recruit Ndamukong Suh to the Los Angeles Rams. Our closer was Mr. Kroenke. We ended up going to one of the most popular restaurants in the entire Los Angeles area, Nobu in Malibu. I didn't know it at the time, but Mr. Kroenke owns a significant amount of land in Malibu. Well, Suh was considering getting a dog at the time. Mr. Kroenke had his dog in Nobu, and it helped lead to a great conversation that eventually closed the deal.

I think about Bill Ford Jr., who runs the Ford Motor Company and was also involved in the ownership group of the Detroit Lions. I think about his humility, how he showed up every day and demanded everyone call him Bill, never Mr. Ford. He'd always go on with stories of his world travel, but he'd always include the lessons he learned and how they could apply to you. He is personable and truly cares about helping others. He has devoted time and financial resources in many areas around the city of Detroit.

I think about so many people I've met. One of my high school coaches, Dan O'Brien, taught me the importance of pride, respect, and paying attention to detail. Take pride in yourself and the work you do. Always have respect for others and yourself, and pay attention to detail. The details truly matter. Whenever we email each other we still sign PRPATD (Pride, Respect, Pay Attention To Detail) at the bottom.

As we invest our daily deposits that lead to our daily systems, the lessons that we can learn from the previous chapters can be applied in so many areas, not just sports, but in business and our home lives. As husbands, fathers, wives, mothers, sons, and daughters, whatever our role is in life, we can learn to become better versions of ourselves by leaning into these simple processes. The challenge is to do it today and every day moving forward. Start stacking your daily habits today.

Unexpected Lessons

I believe leadership lessons can be found in many settings. Perhaps one of the best areas to look is within your own family life. Many positive and negative lessons have been learned when we reflect on seemingly random times in our lives. One of these times for me takes us to the Cape May-Lewes Ferry. This ferry carries passengers and their cars from Cape May, New Jersey, to Lewes, Delaware. This is an 85-minute cruise that takes you across the Delaware Bay.

I am privy to this information because of a faithful Memorial Day Weekend trip that our family took a couple of years ago. Our family had decided to take a quick weekend trip to the Outer Banks in North Carolina. We've always loved the Carolinas, and the Outer Banks are located relatively close to our home in New Jersey. We mapped it out, and it was approximately a six-hour drive to our destination. The family was excited and ready; we even decided to bring our dog, Dublin, along for the journey.

We left on a Friday morning. Before we even pulled out of the driveway, the trip had a rather strange beginning. As I was about to back out of our garage, we noticed something in the driveway. A huge snapping turtle was sitting right in the car's path. Our house is located near a large pond, and we had seen turtles in the area before. After I climbed out of the car and confirmed this was, indeed, a massive snapping turtle, the rest of the family, including Dublin, jumped out to investigate. As I contemplated the best method to move this snappy little critter, I realized that this was not a job for my hands. So, I quickly grabbed a shovel and gently slid the creature out of the way—but not before he got a few big chomps of air that were directed at me. The kids screamed, and Dublin had some words for that turtle, but overall, we escaped the situation unharmed (so did the turtle).

Our focus shifted back to heading to the highway. The plan was to let me drive for the first hour and then switch with Robin so that I could take a Zoom call in the passenger seat. We pulled into a gas station to fill up and switch shortly into our trip. My Zoom call went well and took about an hour and a half. I had my headphones in and was locked into the meeting. The kids were being especially good and keeping the noise level low for me while I actively engaged in the meeting. As we began to wrap up the meeting and the other members logged off, I looked up and noticed a sign that I was not expecting to see at that point. It stated that the ferry lane was beginning ahead.

As I took my earbuds out and further took in the surroundings, I quickly understood that we were approaching a long line of cars awaiting the ferry that would take us into Delaware. We approached the worker at the booth, and my wife explained where we were going. She asked how we could avoid getting on the ferry and save the 85-minute detour. The kind gentleman empathetically explained that if we wanted to drive around and avoid this boat trip, it would add three hours to our trip.

I always attempt to make the best of every situation and consider myself a true optimist. However, I will humbly admit that in that brief moment of learning our fate was taking us on an hour-and-a-half detour, on a boat, with a family, and dog, I did not react well internally. I did a decent job of keeping my cool externally and didn't say any "fun" words in front of the kids. However, inside, I was not a happy camper.

We pulled up and parked in the waiting line, and the next hit came. We would have to wait about an hour for the next ferry to arrive. This is when the self-talk started. Thankfully, when I teach the lessons contained in this book, I am mostly talking to myself. Through years of applying these tactics, I have become an active user of simple actions like adapting. Telling myself to control what I could at that moment helped me to see the situation for what it was. And zooming out to see the entirety of the scenario helped me to refocus and grasp the potential of the moment.

Small moments like this are what we typically reflect on when reminiscing as a family, and I thought this could potentially become one of those moments. We found some areas at the port where the kids could play and enjoyed our time together. When the ferry arrived early, we pulled the car onto the ship and parked. Then we took the kids and Dublin to the upper deck, where they all had a snack. We sat on a bench outside, taking in the views and enjoying the moment. A very kind employee approached us and gave the kids some souvenirs and information about the ferry. She said she liked to pick one family each week to give these things to. She'd chosen us because we looked like we were having so much fun. Zoom out, check. Zoom in, check. Remaining humble and not freaking out when something didn't go our way, double-check.

We arrived in Delaware and disembarked with the family, ready to continue the adventure we had planned. The trip ended up going great; we saw where the Wright brothers' first flight took place and enjoyed nights on the beach with great weather. When my family and I look back at that trip, everyone talks about that ferry. We look fondly at those moments that created a lifetime's worth of memories. We laugh when we think about that first reaction when we all learned that we were in a ferry line. While I could write another chapter about how our phone's map should be clearer about the shortest distance containing a trip on a ferry, I will use my urgent optimism to keep this about the happy memories that were created on Delaware Bay for our family. From beginning to end, this situation became a great memory because we chose to be where our feet were. Lessons from situations like this teach us to adapt and embrace the things that could otherwise distract us from recognizing the opportunity that lies within.

Change and Time

As I continue to reflect on some of the amazing leadership lessons I have learned so far in my life, I travel in my mind to Slovenia. This may seem like an odd transition in a lesson on leadership and personal growth. However, near the border of Italy lies the Postojna Cave Park in Slovenia. This cave system lies in a unique area of Europe located near roads leading not just to Italy but also to Croatia, Hungary, and Austria. It contains the world's first underground train railway, which was opened in 1872. As you travel by small train cars into the underground, the natural beauty consumes you. The rock formations stretch on for miles as the vastness shows you that just below the surface of the earth, a truly amazing scene exists. What can this cave teach us about personal development? As we embrace the lesson of building our daily disciplines through the deposits that we invest in ourselves, it reminds me of the amazing stalagmites that exist in this subterranean climate.

During a recent visit, my wife, Robin, and I visited this cave system. As our tour guide began to drop incredible bits of knowledge about the cave, one thing hit me. It was a drop of water on my head—or several. In this amazing structure, the climate is incredibly wet and around 55 degrees Fahrenheit. As the tour guide described how the floor-dwelling stalagmites form, it reminded me of the daily deposits that we all put into our lives. Each time a tiny drop of water drops on the rocky surface, it allows a microscopic change to take place within the structure. These changes are not visible to even the sharpest human eye, but over time, they create a formidable stalagmite that can stand several feet high. Some of the larger formations inspire awe as you realize that the tiny drops of water have been working on developing the shape since the same time the great pyramids were being constructed. The tiny drops, while not impressive individually, add up to create something with the strength to withstand thousands of years of changing environments.

Here's an explanation of what the heck a stalagmite is and how it differs from a stalactite. Fun fact from the NOAA Ocean Exploration website:

"When discussing mineral formations in caves, we often talk about stalactites and stalagmites. A stalactite is an icicle-shaped formation that hangs from the ceiling of a cave and is produced by precipitation of minerals from water dripping through the cave ceiling. Most stalactites have pointed tips. A stalagmite is an upward-growing mound of mineral deposits that have precipitated from water dripping onto the floor of a cave. Most stalagmites have rounded or flattened tips." (Source: oceanexplorer.noaa.gov)

Call to Action

Lessons of Reflection

- Take time to sit down and reflect. Ask yourself these questions:
    - Who are three people who have positively impacted your life?

    _____

    _____

    _____

- What are three of the most important lessons that you have learned in your life?

  _____

  _____

  _____

  _____

- What three lessons would you offer your younger self?

  _____

  _____

  _____

  _____

- If you zoom out and fast forward 20 years, what three lessons do you need to use NOW with urgency that your future self will thank you for?

  _____

  _____

  _____

  _____

The lessons in this chapter will hopefully allow you to see areas in your own life that offer great learning opportunities. We can learn from others, and we must learn from others. This world is filled with lessons; we must develop the ability to zoom out and see them. Then, the most important step is applying action to these lessons. We must ACT to become the best version of ourselves. You are too important not to invest in yourself!

Conclusion

As we conclude this book, my main challenge is to develop a mindset that defaults to urgency. We all have a call to become better versions of ourselves, and if we approach life with an urgent attitude, we will fulfill that calling. We can do this with several tools discussed in this book, including zoomability. How often do you zoom out and zoom back in?

Disassociate from your negative emotions and allow yourself to see the entire picture with clarity. Continue to use humility and apply it to your daily life. Following through with humility habits will help you develop gratitude, see the perspectives of others, and apply empathy every day. Continue to look at life as if you are exploring a museum rather than rushing through an airport.

I thank you for taking the time to dive into this book, for reading it, and for applying these lessons and action items to your daily life. I hope that you find simplicity in these methods, that you find the actionable items to be exactly that—actionable—that you take the toe test every day, that you wake up with a default attitude of urgency, and that you apply these lessons to your life because you know without a shadow of a doubt that they will lead to better outcomes for you in the future.

What's next, and what's possible? These are exciting questions. The future YOU will thank you for instilling daily deposits today which will lead to a better outcome down the line. Fast forward one, five, or ten years from now, and see yourself as you have applied these daily habits and disciplines into your life. They will lead you to long-term perseverance that will allow you to accomplish great goals and outcomes.

My last bit of advice for you is to hang your daily habits on the STUD.

- The "S" stands for stress. We must learn to lean into adversity and allow the stress to make us stronger. Doing hard things consistently develops physical and mental resilience.

- "T" stands for telescope to microscope. We should practice zoomability every day. Separate from your emotions. See the entire landscape of the situation.

- "U" is for urgency. Default urgent is the attitude we must carry with us. We need to attack life with a tempo of urgency.

- "D" is for daily deposits through disciplined action.

Build the habit of investing in your future self right now. If you haphazardly hammer a nail into drywall and hang something like a valuable picture on it, it will eventually fall and tear that wall apart. However, when we take our time, find the stud, nail into it, and hang our picture on this firm foundation, it will stay mounted for years. And when we hang our daily habits on the STUD, perseverance becomes possible.

Find positive streaks in all three domains: physical, spiritual, and mental. This is part of your daily checklist that will lead to long-term perseverance practices. Did you exercise daily this week? Did you practice prayer or meditation every single day? Are you challenging and stimulating yourself by reading, writing, or consuming podcasts? Continue to challenge yourself. Continue to apply the daily deposits that will lead you to a better outcome.

THANK YOU FOR READING MY BOOK!

DOWNLOAD YOUR FREE GIFTS

Just to say thanks for buying and reading my book, scan the code below for additional resources and a free offering.

Scan the QR Code:

I appreciate your interest in my book and value your feedback as it helps me improve future versions of this book. I would appreciate it if you could leave your invaluable review on Amazon.com with your feedback. Thank you!

www.ingramcontent.com/pod-product-compliance
Lightning Source LLC
Chambersburg PA
CBHW030247010526
44107CB00031B/1352/J